SUCCESSFUL ADVERTISING: KEY ALTERNATIVE APPROACHES

Successful Advertising: Key Alternative Approaches

A management handbook of worldwide principles

Martyn P. Davis BSc (Econ) FCAM FIPR FCIM Dip F Ed

Marketing Communications Consultant

CASSELL

Cassell
Wellington House
125 Strand
London WC2R 0BB

PO Box 605
Herndon
VA 20172

First published 1997

British Library Cataloguing-in-Publication Data
A catalogue record for this book is available from the British Library.

ISBN 0-304-70096-7 (hardback)
      0-304-70097-5 (paperback)

Typeset by Kenneth Burnley at Irby, Wirral, Cheshire.
Printed and bound in Great Britain by Redwood Books, Trowbridge, Wiltshire.

Contents

Preface

The best way to become acquainted with a subject is to write a book about it.

Benjamin Disraeli, onetime British Prime Minister

Many managers hold conflicting views about advertising. Like most people throughout the world, they consider themselves experts at two jobs: their own, and advertising! In consequence, fundamental considerations are overlooked. Even those experienced in advertising often take matters for granted.

At the same time, they are wary of a business discipline which combines the mathematics of media with the creativity of copywriting. This uncertainty is compounded by the terminology involved, which may not be fully understood, and the mystique of advertising agency operations.

Successful Advertising: Key Alternative Approaches gives practical help by taking you step-by-step through the process of planning, executing and evaluating a successful campaign. Every chapter, deliberately kept short to focus attention on each major decision in turn, explains all relevant technical terms, and suggests alternative answers to the crucial questions addressed. These alternatives have been tested not only on innumerable UK business executives but also directly in the many overseas countries where I have mounted Advertising Seminars, and on delegates from more than one hundred countries who over the years attended the International Public Relations Management Summer School where, as Deputy Director, I covered the advertising content.

The Alternatives Approach is a practical tool for any manager responsible for advertising, either direct or through an advertising agency. It will also help those representing media owners or advertising services to better appreciate advertisers' needs, thus improving their selling skills. It is of equal relevance to those preparing for academic or professional qualifications having an advertising content. Finally, the book could also serve as a refresher course for experienced agency personnel.

Successful Advertising: Key Alternative Approaches is intended for worldwide markets and focuses on universal principles. Although these apply internationally (subject, of course, to adaptation for local conditions) this is not a book on international advertising as such. The principles nevertheless apply to international campaigns, just as much as domestic ones.

The principles have universal application in another sense as they are relevant to both products and services, in both consumer and business-to-business markets. They are equally applicable to government, charity or other non-profit campaigns.

The principles are universal in a further sense in that they apply to firms both large and small – although they may not be applied so efficiently. In this respect, large firms have no monopoly of expertise: many small organizations plan most expertly, whereas some large firms often take matters for granted and thus overlook fundamental considerations.

All examples are generic (e.g. 'toothpaste' or 'industrial security systems') rather than named brands, since few companies, products or services are truly international and, for the very few which are, not all readers will recognize ПЕПСИ-КОЛА* for what it is. Readers would not recognize cited campaigns not mounted in their own languages and countries and, furthermore, specific advertising examples date all too swiftly.

Advertising media are also treated generically since they (and their audiences) differ between countries, even though the underlying principles of media selection and planning remain the same and are examined in depth.

Actual media costs and audience data are similarly omitted, since it is impracticable to quote local figures relevant to all readers on a worldwide basis. Furthermore, even if this were possible, current figures (like advertisements) date very quickly.

Each chapter carries an apposite quotation. Disraeli's comment is only partially true, however – I did not learn *The Alternatives Approach* from writing this book, but from working with clients and the thousands of business executives from this country and abroad who over the years attended advertising seminars I directed. What writing this book has done is to codify the alternatives into a single volume.

MARTYN P. DAVIS

---

*PEPSI-COLA in the Cyrillic alphabet.

Acknowledgements

Blessed is he who expects no gratitude, for he shall not be disappointed.

W. C. Bennet, American clergyman, quoted in *The Official Rules* by P. Dickson

Certain individuals merit public thanks – whether or not they expect it!

- Maria Champion for her most helpful comments on the manuscript.
- Alan Cooper, Head of Account Planning at Simons Palmer and Chairman of the Account Planning Group, for reviewing the book at manuscript stage rather than waiting for the printed volume.
- Nigel Moss for his advice on the book's structure, and help with quotations.
- Archie Pitcher, Executive Director – International Advertising Association, for providing the Foreword.
- Naomi Roth, Director of Professional Publishing at Cassell PLC, for her encouragement and, in particular, suggesting that I select suitable quotations to head each chapter – a task I much enjoyed! The many individuals quoted are too numerous to list but, should anyone seek a more specific citation, the author and publishers will be pleased to make the necessary arrangements at the first opportunity. In the meantime, my sincere thanks.
- Dan Yadin of Daniel Yadin & Associates for his constructive critique.
- Finally, my special thanks to the thousands of business executives in this country and abroad on whom *The Alternatives Approach* was tried and tested.

MARTYN P. DAVIS

Terminology

A good terminology is half the game.

Quoted by Arthur Koestler in his *Bricks to Babel*

This book uses general terms such as 'advertiser', 'product' and 'purchaser' for reasons of simplicity. 'Advertiser' may refer to a manufacturer, retailer, service organization or even a non-profit government department; 'product' implies services as well as goods, and 'purchaser' may mean an industrial or governmental organization just as much as the man or woman in the street.

Other general terms refer to media, again for simplicity. Advertisement 'size' includes all variations of the concept and thus covers the length of television or radio or cinema commercials, just as much as press and poster media. Similarly, 'insertions' includes transmission of commercials or any other form of advertisement appearance.

References to advertising 'copy' cover the spoken just as much as the printed word, and 'illustration' includes moving as well as static images.

Unless specifically stated, all media and creative terms should be interpreted as broadly as possible.

Within the main body of the book, I have deliberately avoided references to 'above-the-line' and 'below-the-line' media, since these may not be understood in other countries. For UK readers, however, the terms originate from a line drawn in financial records to separate media-owners who paid commission from those who did not. The phrase above-the-line applies to the five media (press, television, radio, cinema and outdoor) which do pay commission, bookings for which were therefore placed via advertising agencies. Below-the-line media pay no commission, and were usually handled in-house. The term is fast becoming obsolete however, as some agencies now specialize in below-the-line media, or even operate 'across the line'!

I have also deliberately omitted any Glossary, since technical terms are better explained in context – hence the comprehensive Index.

The reader is often addressed as 'you' to avoid references to specific job titles in particular types of organization. Whether your concern is selling advertising space or time, or creating campaigns on behalf of an advertiser or agency, the underlying principles remain the same: you simply approach them from different standpoints. Where specific posts are mentioned, jobs are sometimes described as being held by men: this is again for simplicity and to avoid cumbersome politically-correct phraseology, rather than any male chauvinism or discrimination.

Foreword

As we approach the Millennium, the structure of the advertising, marketing and media business is undergoing rapid and fundamental change. The increasing use of multi-media continues to blur and often eliminates above- and below-the-line concepts.

Agencies are re-examining how best to supply their clients' communication needs; and many advertisers are taking some tasks, particularly Direct Response supervision, back 'in house'.

Martyn Davis's book is a timely reminder that disciplined planning is the key to successful campaigns both nationally and internationally.

The measurement of success and effectiveness is a difficult business. This book points up the fact that, despite these difficulties, clear vision and objective assessment pay off in every market.

It deserves wide distribution and usage.

ARCHIE PITCHER CBE, FCAM, FIPA, FCIM*
Executive Director – International Advertising Association

---

*Archie Pitcher is past President of Ogilvy & Mather Ltd, London, and past World President of the International Advertising Association.

He is also President of CAM – the Communications Advertising and Marketing Education Foundation which he served as Chairman for 12 years. He is a Fellow of the Institute of Practitioners in Advertising, The Chartered Institute of Marketing, The Institute of Directors, and CAM.

How to use this book

When all else fails, follow the instructions.

Service engineer's advice to customer

Planning effective advertising must be treated in the same way as other business tasks – evaluating the situation, deciding objectives, considering alternative ways of achieving them, selecting and implementing the best, and evaluating results. Managers who accept that advertising planning demands as much attention as other business functions ask the crucial questions on which successful advertising depends.

Successful Advertising: Key Alternative Approaches therefore takes you step-by-step through the process of planning, executing and evaluating a successful campaign. Each chapter, deliberately kept short to focus attention on each key planning stage, suggests alternative solutions from which to choose.

On arrival at a T-junction, you have two choices – turn left or right (assuming, of course, you know where you are going, and have no wish to return to the point from which you started!). *Successful Advertising: Key Alternative Approaches* treats advertising planning the same way. It examines alternative advertising objectives and presents alternative answers (summarized in 'boxes' at the head of each chapter) to the vital questions which underly all effective advertising.

In some instances, if not suggesting solutions, the chapters draw attention to alternative considerations which influence advertising decisions, just as your choice at a T-junction might be determined by the state of the roads (good or bad).

These alternative possibilities (usually as unperceived as the questions themselves) lead in turn to different advertising campaigns, with different messages addressed to different markets through different media.

There are even alternative meanings to the word 'alternative':

a) *Either/And/Or* – where you decide which options apply to your own situation.
b) *Ends of scale* – where you decide where you are on this scale.

Although this approach focuses on fundamental issues, the alternatives do not constitute a restrictive 'strait-jacket'. On the contrary, they liberate the creative process by identifying the real problem to be solved.

Key Alternative Approaches provides a series of trigger concepts to facilitate effective planning and, like all check-lists, is an aid to thought and not a substitute for it!

The book concludes with an additional aid to thought: a blank two-page pro-forma to photocopy and complete before undertaking any new advertising assignment.

Should any critic suggest that *The Alternatives Approach* is theoretical and obvious, I conclude with two further quotations. The first, from Harvard Business School, points out that:

There is nothing more practical than a good theory.

The second, this time from myself, asks:

If *The Alternatives Approach* is obvious, why do so many people get things wrong?

PART 1: Advertising in context

There is a master key to success, with which no man can fail. Its name is simplicity.

Henry Detering, former President of Shell Oil

For many months I toyed with an alternative title for this book – *Advertising Made Difficult** – on the basis of the reaction I would receive should I say to any self-appointed advertising 'expert':

'I know the answer to all your business problems. What I propose is that you spend vast amounts of money buying space in innumerable media, saying lots of things to various people numerous times. Sign here!'

The reaction: instant rejection of the proposal, and a barrage of questions on the lines of:

- Why should we advertise?
- What should we advertise?
- Who to?
- What will we say?
- When?
- Which media to use?
- And how much should we spend?

Once business executives accept that advertising planning *is* difficult (rather than a matter of devising snappy slogans) effective advertising becomes easier to achieve, since attention focuses on the essential elements which underly all successful campaigns.

In short, for advertising to be effective, careful planning must ensure that several factors are right:

- Right products – which people would buy if they knew about them.
- Right people – to whom your product is of interest.

---

*Rejected on the grounds that, although it might look intriguing on a Boardroom table, any business handbook should – like a good advertisement – promise readers a benefit. See Chapter 19!

- Right media – which reach these people effectively .
- Right message – which conveys your product's benefits.
- Right timing – when potential customers are likely to buy.
- Right budget – so you do not spend too much or too little.
- Right distribution – with your goods available for purchase.

This planning of 'rights' is an oversimplification, but makes clear the need for planning. Advertising is not a separate operation divorced from marketing: sales, advertising and other forms of promotion must all be co-ordinated. Careful planning ensures that advertising expenditure is controlled and spent to best advantage, and results in profits which more than pay for the advertising. This book describes how best to achieve such a desirable state of affairs.

This first part establishes the functional advantages which result from buying advertising space or time, rather than relying on word-of-mouth recommendations, editorial references and even your own sales force.

A functional definition

'When I say a word,' Humpty Dumpty said in a rather scornful tone, 'it means just what I choose it to mean – neither more nor less.'

Lewis Carroll's *Through the Looking Glass – and What Alice Found There.* *

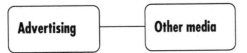

The British Advertising Standards Authority (ASA) once defined advertising as 'The use of paid-for media space or time as a means of persuading people to take a particular course of action, or to reach a point of view.'

The ASA's *British Code of Advertising and Sales Promotion* is now broader in coverage, but this is still the best functional definition. The key words are 'paid-for media', as an essential element in effective advertising is contractual relationships with media-owners, who undertake to deliver your advertising message for a given sum of money. The media owners have a legal obligation to transmit your message and you have a legal obligation to pay them for this service.

Any businessman might justifiably argue that satisfied customers were his best publicity and ask why he should spend money on advertising when word-of-mouth recommendation was spreading news of his products. Most certainly any manufacturer benefits from new purchasers learning about his product from established purchasers, and should do all he can to encourage this: much public relations activity has this very aim. Nevertheless, the use of advertising brings functional benefits which make more than worthwhile the expenditure involved.

- *Definite publication* Message delivery as the outcome of public relations activity involves uncertainty that does not apply to paid-for advertising. Whilst news releases can help secure valuable editorial coverage, and 'Third party endorsement' plays a major role in securing customer acceptance, editorial references are necessarily uncertain, being beyond your control. Should events of greater

---

*Strictly speaking, you have 'alternatives' only if there are just two options. This quotation permits a wider choice!

importance occur, your news release, however well written and targeted, will be spiked. With paid-for advertising you are certain your message will be delivered. (Except, of course, for very occasional strikes, power failures and production problems – nothing is ever 100 per cent certain!)

- *Complete delivery*   On many occasions you will find that, although media have carried your story, editors have 'subbed' the news release rather than print it in full. Word-of-mouth recommendation is similarly unreliable: those who purchase may, in spreading the word, perhaps omit key product features. The same argument applies to sales staff: at the end of a long day on the road, it is unrealistic to expect tired representatives to deliver every sales point. With advertising, you know your message will be delivered in full, simply because you pay media-owners to undertake this very task.

- *Accuracy*   Word-of-mouth recommendation and news releases share a common failing, in that messages may be distorted. With press advertising, you decide precisely which words to use and control how they are presented. Furthermore, you receive proofs to check for accuracy. You have equal control of other media.

- *Timing*   Personal recommendations, valuable though they are, spread haphazardly over time. Equally it is uncertain when (and indeed if) the media will carry your news release. Advertising, on the other hand, can stimulate your market whenever necessary. This may be a matter of months, promoting winter goods in the winter and summer goods in the summer, or alternatively a matter of days, giving a timely boost on a given day of the week.

- *Frequency*   Editorial references may appear only when you have news to release – how are you to stimulate your market in the meantime? Many manufacturers, particularly those with repeat-purchase products, cannot rely on news releases or word-of-mouth. Their products are bought regularly and they need to stimulate the market at appropriate intervals: advertising can do just this, simply by booking regular appearances as part of the campaign plan.

- *Speed*   Advertising communicates rapidly: manufacturers launching new products need an early return on their investment, while others must react swiftly to competition. They rely on advertising to achieve this, rather than the gradual build-up which word-of-mouth or editorial references may bring.

- *Selectivity* Personal recommendations spread indiscriminately: word often spreads to people with no interest in your product. Advertising can be selective, and aimed at those most likely to buy your product.

- *Economy* Advertising costs spread over a very wide range but, whatever the figure, cost per contact is low in comparison with personal selling. One way to spread word about your products would be to increase your sales force, but this would be most uneconomic: salesmen's time is measured in tens of pounds per call, whereas advertising contacts are measured in pennies per thousand. Not only is advertising a more economic way of spreading messages, it can also make your sales executives more productive – paving the way before they make their calls, or providing direct sales leads.

Compared with other communications media, paid-for advertising has the advantages of definite delivery, completeness, accuracy, frequency, speed, timing, selectivity and economy, and – to some extent – all advertising media offer these advantages. Which media you should use, and how best to use them, are discussed later.

Your next step
Having established functional reasons for spending money on advertising, it is essential to assemble all the information on which successful advertising planning depends.

PART 2: Situation analysis

It is a capital mistake to theorise before one has data.

Sherlock Holmes to Dr Watson in Arthur Conan Doyle's *A Scandal in Bohemia*

For advertising to play its part effectively, the first step is to assemble all the information on which successful planning depends.

Whilst there are as many briefing methods as there are people, the approach outlined here has one thing in its favour – it is probably the shortest ever written! Rather than an extensive list of questions, it comprises the eight trigger topics listed below – each of which brings to mind innumerable questions about their inter-relationships and important points of detail. It is important to explore the situation from every angle – far better to gather some irrelevant facts, which may later be discarded, than perhaps overlook a key attribute on which your campaign could be based. These trigger topics are discussed in the following chapters:

Chapter 2 – Your firm
Chapter 3 – Your product or service
Chapter 4 – Your market
Chapter 5 – Your marketing policy
Chapter 6 – Previous activity
Chapter 7 – Constraints
Chapter 8 – Competition
Chapter 9 – Background

And finally:
Chapter 10 – Where to begin?

2 Your firm

The mechanics of running a business are not really very complicated when you get down to essentials. You have to make some stuff and sell it to somebody for more than it cost you. That's about all there is to it, except for a few million details.

John L. McCaffrey, former President of International Harvester

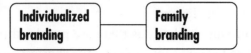

For many consumers, the company which makes the products they purchase is a prime consideration, and the 'sourcing' of industrial products is of equal importance. In consequence, many advertising messages reassure potential purchasers in this respect.

A full knowledge of your firm is essential:

- Is it old-established so that emphasis could be placed on tradition, or a newly-formed pioneer?
- What specialist expertise or facilities might your advertising feature, quite apart from product details?
- Does your firm hold a Royal Warrant, official appointment as sole supplier to a prestigious organization, or some other public recognition?
- Do you have access to the management services and skills of a parent company?
- Is sufficient finance available to mount an extensive advertising campaign?
- Are you, in fact, a single organization or a range of self-contained divisions?
- Do these individual profit-centres operate nationally, on a pan-European basis, internationally or multi-nationally?
- How are their activities co-ordinated?
- Does some corporate theme link them together? If so, this should surely be reflected in your own advertising.

Organizational structure can influence two alternative considerations – are your products marketed individually or under the company's family brand?

Examples of family branding are food producers who market an extensive range of products under a single company name, and the same practice applies in areas such as electronic equipment and domestic appliances.

The reverse is true of the tobacco and brewing industries, where buyers of cigarettes or beer purchase individual brands apparently unconnected with any parent company, whose name they might not even recognize.

Companies which market to the public under individual brand names nevertheless often adopt family branding in their relationships with the trade. Distributors will usually welcome the launch of a new product by a leading company with a wide portfolio of successful brands – the result: ready availability for purchase by consumers, when the advertising campaign breaks on the public.

Ideally, campaigns for any one product or division should benefit the others. All too often, however, there is fragmented marketing effort. At worst, conflicting promotional activities are counter-productive, undermining each other's effectiveness. Alternatively, the various campaigns are merely self-contained, and fail to capitalize on a 'synergistic' approach whereby careful co-ordination actually increases their individual effectiveness and thus that of the overall campaign.

With individualized branding, this synergistic approach is clearly not possible, but the promotional activities of one product or division should nevertheless not undermine the others – imagine competing with colleagues (rather than rivals) for television time or advertising space!

Clearly these considerations affect not only the size and type of your advertising campaign but also its content, so a thorough knowledge of these different aspects is essential.

Your next step

With a thorough knowledge of your firm, the next step is to investigate the product or service to be advertised.

3 Your product or service

There is little that can be said about most economic goods. A toothpaste does little but clean teeth. Aspirin does little but dull pain. Alcohol is important mostly in making people more or less drunk . . . There being so little to be said, much to be invented.

John Kenneth Galbraith, Emeritus Professor of Economics at Harvard University, in his *Economics, Peace and Laughter*

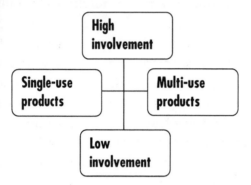

Full details of your products or services (both individually and over the complete range) play an important part in determining advertising messages and media. Colour, container, country of origin, design, ease of operation, guarantees, method of manufacture, name, packaging, price, product range, quality control and after-sales service can all be important. The service element may well be more important than the product itself, as far as users are concerned. Perhaps you provide a service as such, and your firm is a service organization rather than a manufacturing company.

One consideration often (surprisingly!) overlooked is 'What does your product actually do?'. Two alternatives present themselves – does your product have a single use, or do you market a multiple-use product?

Sales of multi-use products can be increased by campaigns which convey their many applications, whereas the advertising of single-use products may be targeted at persuading existing users to use more. Both categories might also seek to persuade purchasers of rival products to switch brands.

As example of a single-use product, can any reader suggest additional uses for toothpaste? There are in fact several: it is very good for cleaning jewellery, can fill small holes in the wall, and doubtless many ingenious other uses could be devised. Situation analysis established earlier the need to discard irrelevant information when selecting the key attribute on which to base your campaign – and the truth of this statement now becomes apparent! Few readers (if any!) would recommend advertising toothpaste on a copy platform that claimed 'Our brand cleans jewellery as well as your teeth, and you can even use it for do-it-yourself repairs!'

So what could you say to increase sales of toothpaste (or any other single-use product, to avoid 'inventing' things as Galbraith suggests? Two alternatives present themselves. One is to suggest that existing users use more – advice to brush your teeth after every meal, and spend at least two minutes brushing, would certainly increase consumption. Alternatively, you could give good reasons why purchasers of rival toothpastes should switch brands and buy yours instead.

Sales of multi-use products on the other hand could be increased by 'recipe' advertisements which point out additional uses for the product. As example, a leading adhesive manufacturer increased sales by promoting 'The A to Z of Things to Stick'. The promotion also cross-referred to other adhesives in the range, thus increasing sales even further.

Some manufacturers make the understandable error of thinking their product a single-use one when in fact it has multiple applications. Cameras and film have but a single function – to take photographs – but the brand leader correctly promoted the memories theme. Postage stamps are similarly marketed as collectors' items as well as functional delivery devices. Numerous products are advertised in their alternative role as gifts, rather than for purchasers' own use.

Two other important alternatives are whether your products call for high or low involvement decisions (both discussed below), since these considerations directly affect your target market's purchasing patterns and in consequence your advertising objective.

Your next step

With a sound knowledge of your firm and its products, the next step is to investigate potential purchasers.

4 Your market

The consumer is not a moron. She is your wife. Respect her intelligence.

David Ogilvy, *Confessions of an Advertising Man*

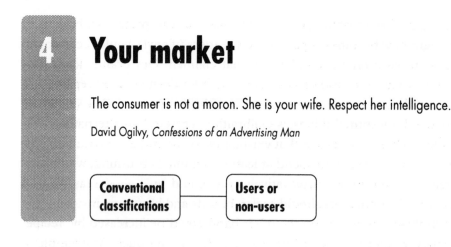

There are numerous ways to classify your target market but, before considering alternative approaches, consider the conventional classifications, variations of which are found in most countries of the world, adapted for local conditions.

Demographics

Effective media planning targets the demographics of your potential purchasers, who may be defined in terms of age, sex and socio-economic groupings. Alternatively your potential customers may be distinguished by a common interest, whether of race or creed, sport or hobby, or product ownership. Manufacturers of business-to-business products, on the other hand, define their target markets differently, in terms of occupation and industrial classifications.

Important considerations for both consumer and business-to-business campaigns are frequency and value of purchase, and geographic location, which influence both messages and media.

A major difference between consumer and business campaigns is that, for the latter, communication is with a small number of potential purchasers. This smaller number, which may be concentrated in a limited number of locations, reach their buying decisions in a different way from purchasers of consumer products (as discussed in Appendix B).

Psychographics

To create persuasive messages, it is equally important to consider psychographics and target market behaviour. Why do people buy your (or your competitors') product, and how do they decide between one brand and another? How strong is their brand loyalty? Who makes the purchase, who influences the buying decision, and does this imply high or low involvement – two considerations raised in the last chapter.

When purchasing low-involvement products (such as a chocolate bar) incorrect decisions do not result in tragedy! With high-involvement products, on the other hand, prospective purchasers will be wary of advertising claims and statements by sales staff, or even editorial endorsements. Accordingly they may well consult people they *do* believe – those who have already made the purchase. In such cases your advertising objective will be to reassure previous purchasers, since they can have a crucial influence on others.

Geodemographics

Another way of classifying your market is in geodemographic terms, by the areas and types of homes in which they live. To give a simple example, there is little point in advertising lawn mowers to people without gardens! By identifying existing customers who live in neighbourhoods with similar characteristics, advertisers can identify potential customers with similar needs.

There are a number of geodemographic systems. One well-known analysis classifies the UK population into 54 neighbourhood types which identify variations in lifestyle, purchasing and expenditure patterns and exposure to different advertising media. Other geodemographic classifications take into account a variety of consumer characteristics.

Lifestyle classifications

Other techniques distinguish potential buyers from non-buyers by classification of personality types. By gathering comprehensive information about attitudes, interests and activities, lifestyle analysis produces consumer behaviour profiles which many claim delineate 'real live people' in a superior way to traditional classifications. Such analyses not only assist media selection, but also provide additional creative input.

Sagacity groups

This method of classifying consumers breaks the population into groups according to whether they are 'blue or white collar' in the dependent, pre-family, family or late stage of life. In the last two stages respondents are also classified as better-off or worse-off, thus making 12 groups in all. Each is designed to be as homogenous as possible, and contain respondents at similar stages of their life cycle, with similar disposable income and cultural characteristics. The various sagacity groups exhibit different behaviour patterns over a wide range of markets, in terms of both media habits and product usage. Different groups, for example, may earn similar salaries but have very different disposable incomes, which they spend in very different ways.

Alternative classifications

Whichever primary classifications you adopt, it is advisable to further divide all markets into two categories, one of which then sub-divides. Some campaigns might target non-users for example, while others aim at users who may in turn be classified as light, medium or heavy.

Each category could call for a different advertising campaign. The media selected to target non-users may differ from media which cover those already using the product. There could similarly be a need for different messages. A campaign aimed at non-users is likely to be educational in approach, explaining the product's benefits to those unaware of them. Other campaigns could aim to turn light users into medium, medium into heavy, or re-inforce heavy users' brand loyalty. These messages would in turn depend on whether the product is single-use (explaining why purchasers should use more) or multi-use (suggesting additional product uses).

When applying this approach to your own products, always remember your market's basic demographic and psychographic characteristics. Certain individuals could be permanent non-users (vegetarians will not eat meat products, for example) while some heavy users might be 100 per cent brand loyal to competitors – you have better uses for advertising money than targeting either group!

Media usage

An extension of the non versus light versus medium versus heavy users approach leads logically to classifying buyers and potential buyers by their *media* habits and attitudes. As example, the easiest way to define a fashion-conscious woman is 'one who reads fashion magazines'. Many firms which classify their markets in terms of product usage apply the same thinking to their use of media – are the target groups heavy, medium, light or non-users of television, radio, newspapers, magazines or other media?

Advertisers can now link target markets with media audiences by relating them to *media imperatives* groupings, which break the population down into four quartiles according to their media preferences. Some men, for example, watch a great deal of television and are also heavy readers of newspapers, others are more exposed to one media group than the other, while some men are difficult to reach through either medium. In this way, the market can be divided into four *media preference groups*:

- *Dual high* (heavy exposure to both media).
- *TV preference* (more exposure to TV than print).
- *Newspaper preference* (those who read more than they view).
- *Dual low* (those with little exposure to both media).

These media preference groups, when related to heavy, medium, light or non-usage of products, can be a most useful aid to media selection and planning.

Knowledge of these many market factors is vital if advertising planning is to be effective. Unless you know and understand your existing and potential purchasers, you cannot select media to reach these people, nor create persuasive advertisements.

Your next step

With knowledge of your firm and its products and market, you must now study how your company sells these products to that market: in short, its marketing policy.

5 Your marketing policy

Everyone lives by selling something.

Robert Louis Stevenson, *Across the Plains*

With both products and the people who buy them clearly established, the next consideration is the 'mechanics' of purchase and sale. Where your product is available can call for detailed messages listing outlets at which would-be purchasers can buy, or for media covering specified sales areas.

Is distribution even across the country, regionally biased, or perhaps limited to certain areas? Many companies divide their selling territory into areas, and marketing thus comprises a number of individual sales drives. A phased or rolling product launch may spread over time, successively covering one area after another until national (or sometimes international) distribution is achieved. This affects both media and messages, since it calls for heavy initial advertising in appropriate areas during launch periods, followed by reminder campaigns during the months which follow. Even where distribution is nationwide, management may decide to increase sales by pinpointing a particular market segment (as distinct from a geographical area) for special attention.

What is your sales-force structure? How many representatives, and how long does it take to complete their round of calls? Do they call on all retailers, or rely on wholesalers to reach smaller outlets? Or is direct mail or telemarketing used to maintain contact with those whom sales staff cannot visit regularly?

How dominant a role do multiple shops and chains play? Is your product generally available (there is no need to tell people where to buy toothpaste!) or only in selected outlets? The need to feature distributors' names and addresses has a marked influence on both media selection and creative content. It may be necessary, for example, to book large spaces in which to list numerous distributors, or select local media relevant to individual outlets' sales areas.

Two alternatives apply to marketing policy, which in turn determine advertising objectives, messages and media – these are *direct selling* or *indirect distribution*.

A later chapter reviews campaign objectives in detail, but it should already be apparent that when a company sells direct it will seek direct response, and look to advertising to provide sales leads via coupon or telephone enquiries or visits to showrooms.

With indirect distribution on the other hand, when products are available through retailers and wholesalers with no direct manufacturer/customer contact, advertising has a different role. Two further alternatives present themselves – *push* or *pull* approaches.

A pull campaign gives minimal discounts but uses massive consumer advertising to pull merchandise through the distribution chain. Retailers get only a small profit per unit, but the prospect of large sales stimulated by public advertising makes them realize they should stock the merchandise, ready to meet demand. In such circumstances, it is good practice to provide representatives with presentation portfolios featuring specimens of forthcoming advertisements together with an outline media schedule, to assist their selling to retail outlets.

With a push campaign on the other hand, little is spent on public advertising, but heavy merchandising and attractive trade discounts are used to persuade retailers to promote the goods, in view of the large mark-up received for each unit sold.

In practice it is rarely a question of operating at either end of this push-pull scale but at some intermediate point, but clearly such factors determine whether or not to use the trade press and the timing of any retail support campaign.

Your next step

With a thorough knowledge of firm and products, market and marketing policy, you must next study previous advertising.

6 Previous activity

If you could sell your experience for what it cost you, you would have a fortune.

Herbert Prochnow

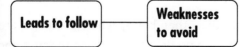

Leads to follow ——— Weaknesses to avoid

Previous activity must be carefully investigated. What advertising has been mounted in the past and with what results? All too often money is wasted through failure to keep adequate records. Careful checking can lead to increased efficiency, bringing better results for the same expenditure or achieving the same results for less outlay. Either way, the benefit is obvious and previous advertising must therefore never be overlooked.

Which advertising media proved effective? What creative approaches appealed to prospective customers? What did these call for in terms of advertisement size, position, colour, frequency, timing and duration of campaign? Has your organization invested time, effort and money over the years in developing a corporate theme or house style which should be continued? You should also investigate other promotional activities that influence buyer behaviour, to ensure that advertising is synergistic with public relations and merchandising or sales promotion.

The alternatives in this case speak for themselves – what favourable advertising 'indicators' should you develop, and which weaknesses should you avoid?

Before planning future advertising you should therefore check what lessons you can learn from the past. In turn, the results of this year's campaign should provide the basis of next year's planning. This preliminary stage of situation analysis thus links directly with the final planning stage of *evaluation of results*, to which a later chapter is devoted.

When launching a new product with no previous promotional activity, a useful preliminary step is to study *candidate media* – those media it seems likely you may use and will later analyse in depth, once you have decided your campaign objective. This concept is discussed further in Chapter 24.

Your next step

Your next task is to identify any restraints which may constrain advertising planning.

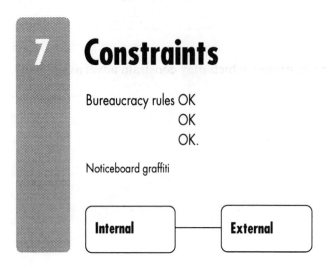

7 | Constraints

Bureaucracy rules OK
OK
OK.

Noticeboard graffiti

Internal ──── External

Constraints that restrict advertising planning can be *internal* or *external.*

Internal

These considerations should come as nothing new but would have arisen under any of the headings just considered, when a 'warning bell' should signal their implications. Your firm, for example, may have financial constraints that restrict advertising expenditure. Is there a limit to the amount you can produce – it is pointless to stimulate demand you cannot satisfy. Some market segments may be permanent non-users, or brand loyal to rival products. Marketing policy can be equally important, calling for media that target particular areas and/or can invite direct response. The need to list local dealers can influence both message content and media choice.

External

Advertising practice is not without external limitations, as numerous legal constraints and self-regulatory systems may restrict your actions. Such limitations vary country by country but, whatever your location, you should investigate both official and voluntary control systems. Within the United Kingdom, for example, advertisers must take account not only of the ASA's self-regulatory *Code of Advertising and Sales Promotion,* but also official advertising regulations imposed by the Independent Television Commission (ITC) as well as separate codes of practice specific to other media. In addition, there is a host of legal and regulatory restrictions on trading practices. Other countries no doubt have similar restraints – or even additional ones covering, for example, joint venture operations between UK companies and their overseas partners.

Clearly your investigations must make you aware of just what you are (and are not) allowed to say and do – how else can you prepare advertising that satisfies these requirements?

Your next step

With possible restrictions clearly established, the next step is to investigate the competition you face from rival firms.

8 Competition

In truth, I don't suppose there's ever been a time when competing products were anything but pretty similar: that's why they are competing products.

Jeremy Bullmore, non-executive director of the Guardian Media Group and WPP Group

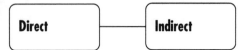

Direct

The competition you face must be reviewed under each heading so far considered. With which firms do you compete? How do their products compare with your own? Who are the purchasers of rival products? How are these products marketed? What advertising campaigns do competitors mount? Finally, what restraints do your competitors face – external constraints such as the ASA's *Code of Advertising and Sales Promotion* affect all equally, but competitors' internal restraints may give you a competitive edge which could feature in your advertising.

Indirect

A clear understanding of indirect competition, which you and rival suppliers face from other product groups, can be equally important – manufacturers of television sets, for example, compete not only with each other but with alternative uses for consumers' money, such as holidays.

On occasion, rival producers find it productive to mount co-operative advertising campaigns for their product group as a whole. Having increased the size of the market for, say, beds or furniture, they then compete – through their individual advertising – for increased slices of the larger cake.

Your next step

It is important to recognize that you – and your competitors – operate against the background of a national economy increasingly influenced by international factors. This must be carefully investigated, before commencing the planning process.

9 Background

Economic forecasting houses . . . have successfully predicted fourteen of the last five recesssions.

David Fehr, former Professor of Finance at Harvard Business School

```
┌─────────────┐     ┌─────────────┐
│  P-E-S-T    │─────│  S-W-O-T    │
└─────────────┘     └─────────────┘
```

Not alternative solutions, but key considerations included for completeness are two acronyms – PEST and SWOT – which facilitate review of the environment in which you (and your competitors) operate.

P-E-S-T

These initials represent four considerations which directly affect your organization's success (or failure): political, economic, sociological and technological:

- *Political* This concerns not which party you vote for, but simply recognizes that political decisions in Westminster or Europe – or indeed other capital cities – directly affect the day-to-day running of any business. Changes in tax structure, capital allowances or development grants all illustrate how political decisions have business implications. Changes in the law can be equally important.
- *Economic* This consideration overlaps the first, since different political parties have different policies for dealing with economic ills such as inflation, recession or unemployment. We must recognize, however, that our economy is influenced by others – action on oil prices, changes in exchange rates, or decisions about interest levels all have far-reaching effects on other countries' standards of living.
- *Sociological* Consider the changing roles of women and young people in our society, the increasing number of single-parent families, general concern about health and environmental issues, changes in shopping habits, or the development of Britain's multi-racial society – all have direct implications for business operations. In some cases, sociological and political changes interact – for example, repeal of restrictions on Sunday trading.

- *Technological* Even if your product is not undergoing a technological revolution, your organization is certainly affected by technological changes, particularly as they affect advertising media. Printing quality has improved for most press media, colour is increasingly available, and copy dates (by which media-owners must receive your advertising material, in advance of publication) are shortening. Television has been revolutionized by satellite and cable, and digital technology already affects radio as well as television. Direct mail has similarly undergone a technological revolution and, to varying degrees, all advertising media have been affected.

S-W-O-T

These initials come from a well-known marketing analysis which has equal application to advertising policy. Bearing in mind the many factors just reviewed and likely future trends, what are your *strengths* and *weaknesses,* and what *opportunities* and *threats* face your organization?

Your next step

Although listed as your first task, situation analysis is in fact a never-ending exercise. Today's events may directly affect both you and your target groups, and markets must therefore be constantly monitored. Many newly-appointed executives recognize that situation analysis never ends: their problem is where to begin.

Where to begin?

With the possible exception of the Equator, everything begins somewhere.

Peter Fleming, *One's Company*

Pareto analysis

How should you set about situation analysis for a business which sells an extensive product range to numerous types of purchasers spread across a large number of markets – or even different countries? One solution is what is known as *pareto analysis* – applying the 80/20 rule based on previous profits.

Some products, purchasers or markets are often more profitable than others, usually in an 80/20 ratio. If 80 per cent of profits come from 20 per cent of your product range, it is logical to concentrate initially on finding out about these particular products. For these selected products, the same analysis can reveal the most profitable markets and target groups. In this way, you identify the relatively small number of big buyers who merit most attention.

The converse is that 80 per cent of your products, purchasers and markets account for only 20 per cent of profits, and pareto analysis can identify the many small buyers making only a limited profit contribution, who merit less attention.

When constructing media plans later, advertising expenditure can then be allocated between the more and less profitable target groups in the same proportions, according to their 'market weights' or values.

Never forget, however, that all markets are necessarily in constant flux. The 80/20 rule is a sound starting point, but its very opposite – 20/80 analysis – can often make an equally positive contribution. Hence the importance of a never-ending study of trends, to identify those products, purchasers or minority markets which, although making only a small profit contribution at present, may be the big earners of the future. Fighting competitors for today's markets should not prevent you from cultivating tomorrow's profitable target groups, which competitors may not yet have identified.

The shotgun approach

Pareto analysis implies that past profit figures are available for analysis, and so is inapplicable for entirely new products. How would you set about planning to launch – with no previous data – a revolutionary new product, highly relevant to a wide range of possible purchasers within many different markets? Conventional research is both costly and time-consuming and, in any event, which market segment would you investigate first? An alternative approach is to formally recognize this lack of data, spend your money on advertising rather than conventional research, use advertising as a research tool, and plan a 'shotgun' campaign. If both purchasers and markets are unknown quantities, it is clearly impossible to mount a focused campaign, so your objective must be to get prospects to identify themselves. Accordingly, your campaign can comprise a large number of small direct-response advertisements spread over a wide range of candidate media. Your initial advertising serves a research function: those market segments which respond clearly merit attention, and future campaigns can be focused accordingly.

Your next step

With situation analysis complete, you now have a firm base on which to plan your advertising strategy.

PART 3:
Deciding your advertising strategy

If you don't know where you are going, you will probably finish up somewhere else.

Mark Twain

With situation analysis complete, you can now start more positive planning. Before creating messages or selecting media, however, it is vital to establish a clear objective. In so doing, you must avoid possible pitfalls:

1. Being too greedy

Throw someone a tennis ball and most people will catch it. A few individuals may catch two tennis balls, but three or more? Some advertising campaigns do indeed achieve more than one objective, but this is achieved by careful planning rather than luck.

2. Being too ambitious

Deciding how much to spend is the next stage in the planning process but, however generous the budget, there is never enough money! Campaign objectives must be realistic – to make *everybody* think well of your company *all the time* is neither achievable nor affordable.

3. Being imprecise

Objectives must be specific. To 'improve your company's image', you need answers to very basic questions:

*   Whose opinions concern you?
*   What opinions do these target groups have now?
*   What opinions do you wish them to hold?

Without answers to these questions, the so-called aim of an improved image has no real meaning.

If your objective is to be measurable, this precision should also extend to numbers and dates – an X per cent shift within Y months, in opinions (or sales) by a specified target group.

4. Creative confusion

Campaign objectives must not be confused with *communication* objectives, which concern a later stage in the planning process – preparation of proposals. Specifying a precise objective is one thing – creating messages to achieve that objective is a quite distinct task.

Chapter 11 discusses possible advertising objectives.

11 Deciding your advertising objective

Management by objectives works if you know the objectives. Ninety per cent of the time, you don't.

Laurence J. Peter

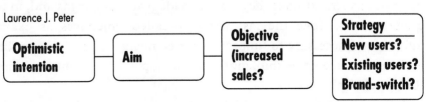

There is an extensive range of possible reasons for mounting a campaign. Those encountered most frequently include – not in any order of importance – the following:

- Remind previous purchasers.
- Reassure existing users.
- Counter the natural decline inherent in any market.
- Inform the constant flow of new customers.
- Inform the market of changes.
- Overcome resistance.
- Launch a new product or service.
- Extend distribution.
- Stimulate existing distribution.
- Provide sales leads.
- Persuade unknown potential purchasers to identify themselves.
- Build up a mailing list.
- Level out variations in sales.
- Strengthen individual product promotions with an 'umbrella' campaign covering your full range.
- Improve your company's image.
- Fight declining sales.
- Increase sales.

The first four objectives should be reviewed together, in recognition of the fact that all markets are in constant flux. They decline steadily through natural causes (which economist Lord Keynes once illustrated by pointing out that 'In the long term we're all dead!') and there are always potential new customers in need of information (those who entered the market for the first time today!). In the meantime, you need to remind previous purchasers or reassure existing users (depending on whether your product necessitates a low or high involvement decision).

The objectives listed are only outlines and must be made specific, to avoid the sad state of affairs against which Laurence J. Peter warns. Inadequate briefings must be challenged since they lead to inadequate campaigns and, in turn, inadequate results. Take the last three so-called objectives as examples. The information necessary to 'improve your company's image' was outlined earlier, and the same precise thinking must be applied to 'Fight declining sales' or 'Increase sales'.

Loose objectives such as 'Fight declining sales' must be avoided, even if with numbers and dates. If sales are falling, *why?* If because of the natural decline inherent in any market, the solution lies in targeting new potential purchasers. Alternatively, are sales falling because users are switching to rival brands? If so, there are clear implications for both creative strategy and media selection. If, however, your product has reached the end of its life cycle, do not expect advertising to work miracles! To counter declining sales, you must first identify why they are falling and then plan your advertising accordingly.

A similarly practical analysis should apply to 'Increased sales' and this is where the difference between *Optimistic intention – Aim – Objective* and *Strategy* becomes important.

A campaign to increase sales is little more than an *optimistic intention*.

The *aim* of: 'Increase Sales of Product A to Target Group B in Area C' gives more guidance but ignores two vital questions – what percentage increase, and by which date? – which a true *objective* would make clear.

For effective advertising, planning should extend even further by specifying the *strategy* by which increased sales are to be achieved – getting existing users to use more, attracting new users, or persuading buyers of rival products to switch brands. These three routes to increased sales could call for different messages and different media to deliver them.

The too-easy solution of an imprecise objective must be avoided if you are to plan effective advertising.

Your next step

The next planning stage is deciding how much to spend on achieving your specified objective.

PART 4:
Deciding how much to spend

Half the money I spend on advertising is wasted. The trouble is, I don't know which half.

Lord Leverhulme

Most firms realize that advertising is a cost which brings savings in its wake. The problem lies not in deciding *whether* to spend money on advertising, but in deciding *how much* to spend.

Whenever I hear Lord Leverhulme's comment, I always recall my visit to the president of a gigantic shopping centre in Midwest America. In reply to my question as to how many people worked at the centre, his laconic reply was 'About half of them.'

You must ensure that *all* your advertising money works for you, and consider your budget in context, as part of a complex business operation. It then becomes apparent that fixing the advertising budget is a *management* decision, and part of a process of balancing expenditures when different activities compete for funds.

It is therefore sound practice to approach budgeting from the standpoint of ROI or ROC (return on investment or on capital) rather then *spending money*. For management to authorize any appropriation, you must convince Directors that advertising, rather than any other use of funds, will be the most productive form of expenditure, and make a positive contribution to profitability. Should your Board view advertising as spending without results, you are unlikely to have any budget approved.

This Part therefore covers:

Chapter 12 – Budgetary methods
Chapter 13 – Contingency reserves.

12 Budgetary methods

The buck stops with the guy who signs the cheques.

Rupert Murdoch, Chairman and Chief Executive of News Corporation

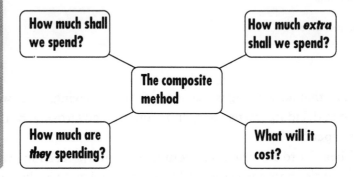

The advertising budget serves as an effective management tool, focusing attention on how, when and where to spend your money. It equally helps control expenditure. This is an important step, since without such a discipline money may be frittered away.

The amount spent on advertising is known as the 'appropriation', and budgetary policy is usually initiated some three months before the start of the marketing year. The term is defined as 'the total amount to be spent on advertising during a given period'. Two points merit clarification – for very practical reasons.

One is budget coverage. How can you prepare a meaningful plan without knowing exactly what your appropriation covers and, perhaps more important, which costs should be covered by *other* departments. Many sad stories illustrate the importance of such clear understanding, all with a common outcome – advertising insertions cancelled to make up the money in dispute, so upsetting a carefully planned schedule, thus removing advertising support when needed, resulting in lost sales which in turn meant loss of profit.

The second equally practical consideration is the length of time to be covered – how can you prepare a plan without knowing the precise period in question, and when it starts and finishes? Most appropriations are for 12 months, some are longer term whilst others cover shorter periods, but the annual appropriation is more usual. Accounting practice often makes this inflexible, so that towards the end of the period you are not allowed to borrow from next year's budget nor carry over any unspent funds.

The numerous ways of establishing an appropriation can be grouped into categories, each with numerous variations. In some cases the arithmetic can be done on the back of an envelope whereas other instances call for a computer to undertake intricate calculations: it is, nevertheless, the same basic method. The fundamental choices open to you are, in outline:

1. How much shall we spend?

Various methods approach budgeting as a percentage costing exercise, based on past or anticipated sales, or on production costings, which indicate a given percentage for each unit produced.

2. How much *extra* shall we spend?

An alternative approach is the marginal or zero-based method. Rather than establish a budget and then decide how to spend it, this method adopts a more pragmatic approach. Those applying it decide their expenditure 'layer by layer', with each advertisement paying its way. Needless to say, not all advertisers can adopt this practice: only the fortunate few able to evaluate results directly, in terms of actual sales.

3. How much are *they* spending?

Some advertisers adopt a competitive parity approach, to ensure they are not outspent by competitors. Some compare actual expenditure figures, whilst others consider 'share of voice' – is their share of total advertising expenditure the same as their market share? This could be unwise, however, if your competitors are not spending their budgets cost-effectively as, in emulating them, you would be wasting money. In any event rivals, although similar to your own organization, are not the same: they have different products and different objectives. Finally, finding out just what competitors are spending is no easy task.

4. How much will it cost?

The target sum or objective-and-task method approaches the problem in a different way, by establishing how much it will cost to do the job. The desired campaign is planned and its cost calculated. In short, this approach reverses the two planning stages of deciding the budget and then devising the campaign. Many public relations budgets are decided this way, and the same approach can be applied to advertising.

Whatever the sequence, the planning stages of specifying objectives, setting budgets and preparing proposals should always be interlinked. This linkage raises the important matter of priorities, as the planning process may not always proceed smoothly. If the desired campaign is unaffordable, then planners must reconsider. Can the campaign be implemented at lower cost by better creativity and media planning? If not, then either the budget must be increased or objectives reduced to a more realistic level. Reality impinges!

5. The composite method

Many practitioners adopt a fifth approach, using two or more methods at the same time. The amounts in question, which in any event are unlikely to be vastly different, indicate maximum and minimum expenditure levels. The range of uncertainty is thus narrowed down in a most practical manner, and it is at this point that situation analysis coupled with experience can tell you where, within the prescribed range, you should fix your own appropriation.

Any reader seeking the impossible – a universally applicable method – will be disappointed. Even if a single ideal method were available, there is considerable difference between fixing a sum and then a) using it and b) spending it. The circular procedure of last year's results helping determine this year's expenditure should be influenced by two later stages in the planning process: preparing and then executing your advertising proposals.

a) When *using* your advertising budget, how strong will your creative proposals be? A powerful selling proposition, made to come alive in a compelling way, will produce results for less expenditure than weak creative proposals.

b) Equally important is the efficiency with which you *spend* your advertising money. A good media buyer, by hard bargaining, will get more for your money or, putting the same thing another way, buy the same amount of advertising for a smaller outlay.

Both aspects are discussed in later chapters.

Budget divisions

Your organization, rather than have a single budget, may require several appropriations, one for each product or division. It may even need an additional budget to finance an 'umbrella' campaign for the group as a whole rather than any individual product.

You may also encounter divisions for yet another reason: to set aside funds for manufacturer/stockist co-operation. Many firms find it productive to share with retailers the cost of local advertising, announcing that they stock the merchandise featured.

Some advertisers also set aside funds as a contribution to co-operative advertising campaigns mounted on an industry-wide basis, to increase demand for their product group as a whole.

Your next step

Before starting preparation of proposals, it is sound practice to set aside a further part of your budget – known as a *contingency reserve* – to cater for unexpected opportunities or setbacks.

13 Contingency reserves

Planning for the change must be the ever-present concern of every single executive.*

Jesse Werner

Pre-planned

Before starting any detailed planning, it is sound practice to consider a contingency reserve. Rather than plan expenditure to the last penny, most advertisers find it advisable to keep some funds in reserve. This spare cash can serve two purposes. On the negative side, it allows for unexpected expenditure which would otherwise make inroads into your carefully planned campaign. On the positive side, reserves allow you to take advantage of unexpected opportunities. In a highly volatile market, it may be desirable to keep back a considerable contingency reserve, while in a stable marketing situation a nominal amount may be quite sufficient. Trial and error over the years can provide valuable guidance as to a suitable size reserve for your own company.

In establishing your contingency reserve, you are in fact trying to predict the unpredictable! This is a difficult decision, for if contingencies are under-estimated and call for more than the amount set aside then you must cancel some advertising to provide the necessary money, and your carefully planned schedule will be ruined. If on the other hand you over-estimate the amount, it is tempting to fritter away this too large reserve at the end of the year, rather than leave it unspent and face criticism from financial staff when seeking budget increases in the future. There is also a danger that this contingency fund might be considered surplus to requirements and 'taken back' when things get tight, thereby removing your ability to make tactical moves.

---

*This quotation applies equally to the 20/80 analysis mentioned earlier, as well as the execution stage discussed later.

On-going funding

Some advertisers take a different approach and, rather than establish a contingency reserve in advance, build one up over the campaign period. Aggressive media buying, while executing the media plan, provides another way of coping with the unexpected, the money saved being used to fund a contingency reserve.

Your next step

With situation analysis complete, a clear objective and the amount available to achieve this objective established, you can now start planning messages and media as discussed in Parts 5 to 8.

Whether you should undertake these tasks in-house or use external services (such as an advertising agency) is discussed in Appendix A.

PART 5: The advertising interlock

Doing business without advertising is like winking at a girl in the dark. You know what you are doing, but nobody else does.

Stewart Henderson Britt

Parts 6 and 7 discuss preparation of message and media proposals. To develop these effectively, however, you must consider them in context, and review how messages and media jointly relate to marketing, and how they in turn interlock with each other. This Part therefore covers:

Chapter 14 – The marketing, message and media interface
Chapter 15 – The message and media interlock.

14 The marketing, message and media interface

Creative thought requires an act of faith.

George Gilder

Marketing strategy	Message content	Media policy
	Six alternative options	

As Part 3 made clear, there are numerous reasons for advertising. This chapter focuses, however, on increased sales since this heads many an agenda. It is also a blind spot, as many executives fail to link messages and media with marketing.

One well-known marketing matrix suggests four ways to increase sales:

- Existing products to existing markets.
- Existing products to new markets.
- New products to existing markets.
- New products to new markets.

These possibilities can then be evaluated against a 'risk' scale, with the fourth clearly being the most risky.

This matrix may assist marketing planning, but is unsatisfactory for advertising purposes since it fails to allow for competition, or consider campaigns which persuade customers to switch brands.

The alternative matrix below facilitates planning both messages and media. A first essential is to stop thinking of increased sales, and instead of increased *purchases* – or, more specifically, possible purchasers and their buying behaviour. Viewed in purchasing terms, there are three ways to increase sales of existing products:

1. *Increased purchases by existing users.* This will increase the value of the market, but not its size in terms of people.
2. *Purchases by new users.* This will increase the size of the market in terms of people, as well as its monetary value.
3. *Purchases by competitors' customers.* This will not increase the size of the market – only the way it is divided.

These three routes to increased sales of existing products facilitate more effective planning than the earlier matrix which recognized only two – existing and new markets – and ignored brand-switch sales.

The alternative matrix does not yet cover new products, so analysis must now extend beyond the three possibilities so far considered. A full planning matrix should also allow for:

4. *Purchases of new products by existing customers* – you know who your customers are and can perhaps reach them through, for example, direct mail. Furthermore, there is (hopefully) a wealth of goodwill to assist in launching your new product.
5. *Purchases of new products by new users* – as the product is new, there is no track record on which to build: the testimonial approach of 'thousands of satisfied users' is inapplicable. Furthermore, there is no goodwill from which to benefit.
6. *Purchases of new products by competitors' customers* – there is again no track record on which to build, and furthermore you must fight established goodwill.

If the new product is a multi-use one, this six-route matrix can be extended by follow-up campaigns which suggest additional product uses – or, for single-use products, reasons for more frequent use. This completes the circle by linking back to the first route to greater sales – *increased purchases by existing users.*

If the increased sales/increased purchases analysis is reduced to a fundamental level, message content and media policy can be summarized as shown in the chart on page 42.

A campaign destined to meet any one objective is unlikely to be as successful in achieving the other five, since all could call for different messages in different media.

From the creative standpoint a campaign aimed at existing users, suggesting further uses for your product, may not be understood by new users unaware of the product's basic function, let alone additional uses. A campaign which explains basic benefits to potential users may bore existing users, already well aware of what your product does. Neither will effectively influence brand loyalty to rival products. Equally, a campaign to persuade competitors' customers to switch brands, stressing the advantages of your product over others, is likely to be unsuccessful in educating new users. Campaigns for new products call for similar core differences in creative content.

The same is true of media policy. To increase sales to existing customers you would clearly continue (but strive to improve) your present media pattern, while to reach new buyers you may have to use new media. Playing 'Follow my leader'

The marketing, message and media interface

Sales increase strategy	Message content	Media policy
Existing products		
1. Existing products to existing users	Suggest new uses for your product or reasons for more frequent use, building on existing contacts and goodwill	Maintain insertions in current media
2. Existing products to new users	Explain your product's basic benefits and your company record to people unaware of them	Consider new media
3. Existing products to users of rival products – brand-switching	Comparison campaigns pointing out the advantages of your products over rival brands, and of changing buying habits	Consider competitors' media patterns
New products		
4. New products to existing customers	Explain basic benefits, building on existing contacts and goodwill	Maintain insertions in current media
5. New products to new users	Explain basic benefits, and company record in other fields	Consider new media
6. New products to competitors' customers	Explain basic benefits and overcome established goodwill	Consider competitors' media patterns

rarely results in effective advertising but, should you seek brand-switch sales, you would deliberately aim at your competitors' market – and are thus likely to use the same media. This is very different to blindly following your rival's lead for lack of anything better to do.

Advertising must therefore be based directly on clear and detailed marketing objectives.

Different routes to increased sales can call for different messages as well as different media. Like most fundamental truths these alternatives are very obvious – once they have been pointed out! They are, nevertheless, far too common a blind spot for many managers.

Of course, the matrix over-simplifies for ease of analysis and, furthermore, in practice is not as easy as simply delivering Message A to new users through Media A, Message B to existing users through Media B, and Message C through Media C to persuade people to switch brands. However tightly you target both messages and media, there will always be overlap.

Finally, the six types of increase are not self-exclusive and there certainly are advertisements which increase sales in two or more ways simultaneously. Many successful campaigns recognize the distinct routes to increased sales and accordingly comprise inter-related components, each aimed at one distinctive target group. These are not only successful in their own right but, because they are clearly linked, each component reinforces the others. Synergistic advertising such as this is achieved by design, never by accident.

There are of course many objectives other than increased sales: all call for equally specific messages and media.

Your next step

With their relationship to marketing clearly established, the next step is to ensure that messages and media interlock.

15 The message and media interlock

When you accept our views, we shall be in full agreement with you.

Moshe Dayan of Israel to Cyrus Vance of USA, 10 August 1977

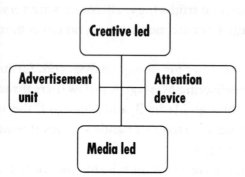

As any advertising campaign represents a combination of messages and media, broad agreement must be reached on two inter-related decisions before developing either aspect in detail.

1. The advertisement unit

The decision to book, say, colour pages in women's magazines is two decisions in one. It is a creative decision to prepare full-page colour advertisements for the women's press and, at the same time, it is a media decision to plan a schedule whereby colour pages will be booked in selected women's magazines at a given cost. Creative staff must accept that this gives full scope to convey the product's benefits persuasively, and media staff accept it as the basis for effective scheduling.

The possibility of agreement on more than one size of advertisement unit is discussed in Chapter 28.

2. Attention device

Creative and media must also agree on another important point of principle – how to attract attention. It is insufficient to create effective advertisements and then simply place them in suitable media (however persuasive or efficient either campaign element may be) in the hope that people will see them. Positive action must ensure that advertisements not only appear but are actually *seen*.

There are various ways to attract attention, both by creative and media means. Media methods include front-page or solus advertisements, and special positions facing editorial. Other routes to attention are purely creative, including arresting headlines and eye-catching illustrations. Some attention devices have implications for both creative and media staff, who will equally welcome colour and large sizes, but for different reasons. Whatever the means of attracting attention, creative and media agreement is essential. This need applies equally to all media groups likely to feature in the final schedule.

For simplicity, future references to advertisement unit cover both aspects of these inter-related message/media decisions.

Media or creative led?

In reaching these two joint decisions, creative or media consideration may be dominant – and sometimes in conflict. When preparing proposals for a product that benefits from demonstration, creative staff may press for TV or cinema, which offer colour, sound and movement. Media planners may, however, point out that other media provide more effective coverage. Some element of conflict is often unavoidable, but the two sides must nevertheless reach agreement. There is little point in creative staff preparing advertisements for media that do not reach the market, nor media planners preparing schedules which give insufficient creative scope. Similarly, it is pointless for creative staff to demand large sizes when budget limitations rule these out.

Attention in context

Depending on the medium, the battle for attention may be partly won already. It is important to consider, for example, if messages are intrusive or welcome in the medium.

It is equally important, when designing material, not to lose your own battle – many advertisements are cluttered, or have components in conflict.

These aspects of advertising are discussed in later chapters.

Your next step

With advertisement unit (and attention device) agreed, the next task must turn campaign objectives into *communication* objectives, and create arresting and persuasive advertisements.

PART 6: Preparation of proposals – messages

The great art in writing advertisements is finding out a proper method to catch the reader's eye, without which a good thing may pass over unobserved, or be lost among commissions of bankrupt.

Addison, *The Tatler*, No. 224

The three planning stages of situation analysis, objective, and budget summarize the problem, which must be distinguished from possible solutions.

Preparation of proposals is a separate stage in the planning process, and should not be pre-empted by such statements as 'I await your proposals for delivering message A, with full-colour illustration B, through double-page spreads in media C, D and E.'

It is equally important to avoid 'non-instructions' such as 'What I really want is an eye-catching, attractive, interesting and memorable campaign.' Who in their right mind ever seeks to produce unnoticeable, dull, boring and forgettable advertisements?

A third common error is the 'King Kong' approach – most readers will recall either the original black-and-white film or the more recent technicolour version. Many campaigns bring to mind the giant gorilla beating its chest, with the advertiser proudly announcing what he wants to say. Campaign planning should, of course, start at the other end of the communication process – potential purchasers and what they need to know about your product or service.

First define the problem – *then* turn to the next planning stage: preparation of proposals to achieve the defined objective, within the constraints of the budget.

Although the two interlocking components of any campaign – messages and media – are developed in parallel, we turn first to the task of creating arresting and persuasive advertisements. This Part therefore covers:

Chapter 16 – The creative intention
Chapter 17 – The buying decision process
Chapter 18 – Models of communication

16 The creative intention

Pray have on my desk by noon tomorrow, on one side of a sheet of paper, your plans for reconquering Europe.

Winston Churchill, when war leader, to his Armed Forces Commander

Why should the target audience read your advertisement?	Having read it, what is the desired response?

Having defined the problem, rather than proceed direct to full preparation of message proposals, it is good practice to take the interim step of writing a creative intention to outline your suggested solution. Do not write any actual copy, but *prepare* to write. Winston Churchill's practice, when applied to advertising, not only clarifies the mind but saves time and trouble later. If your objective is to be achieved, two key considerations when evaluating a creative intention are:

1. *Why should the target audience read your advertisement?*
Earlier discussion of attention devices made clear that ensuring advertisements are actually seen is a joint creative/media decision. Whatever the attention device, your message must nevertheless still arrest attention in its own right. What will you say, in headline and/or illustration, to lead readers into the text?

2. *Having read your advertisement, your target groups should think, feel or believe what?*
If your advertisement is effective, prospective purchasers may recall one 'big idea' – what is this to be? What single thought or proposition do you want them to recall? And what is the desired response? Do you seek to change attitudes, impart knowledge, or influence behaviour? If the former, distinguish between long-term basic beliefs and current needs. Advertising can influence short-term buying behaviour, but changing entrenched beliefs is a very different matter. If you wish to influence behaviour, what do you want potential purchasers to actually *do*? Functional information can increase response: are phone enquiries free on a 24-hour basis, what are trading hours and how best to reach the showroom?

Approach message planning as a 'creative sandwich', and concentrate initially on the outside 'slices' before devoting many hours to the filling – discussed in later chapters. There is little point in polishing any message until you are clear how you will attract target market attention, and have specified the desired outcome.

Many practitioners argue that a creative intention is as important as actual proposals in ensuring discussion by all concerned, analysis of alternative ways of achieving objectives, voicing and overcoming possible objections, and agreement on overall advertising policy.

This well-founded belief merits a second military quotation:

Gentlemen, there will be no questions as I intend to make everything perfectly clear.
> Field Marshal Lord Montgomery, when briefing senior officers

Apparent exceptions

With 'Teaser' campaigns, the two key questions posed by a 'creative intention' are treated somewhat differently as everything is deliberately *not* made clear. On the contrary, the desired response is to stimulate questions – as many as possible! Coupled with an intriguing reason for prospective purchasers to read the advertisement in the first place, this approach can result in considerable discussion prior to the main campaign in which all is revealed. Some teaser campaigns comprise an extended series of advertisements, for even greater speculation.

Your next step

To reach these two decisions it is often necessary to think ahead and consider your prospect's decision process, and how advertising actually communicates.

17 The buying decision process

When I write an ad I don't want you to tell me that you find it creative. I want you to find it so interesting that you have to buy the product.

David Ogilvy

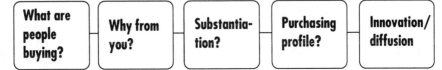

What are people buying?	Why from you?	Substantia-tion?	Purchasing profile?	Innovation/diffusion

Appendix B analyses business-to-business buying decisions in detail. This chapter, however, focuses on key considerations critical to any purchase. These in turn help relate your copy platform to what consumers need to hear, if they are to make sound decisions – to your mutual benefit.

1. *What are people buying?* – as distinct from what you are selling.
A leading beauty products manufacturer commented that 'In our factory we make cosmetics. In our advertising we sell hope.' An example mentioned earlier is that people buy memories rather than cameras and film. Some companies sell industrial power drills, whereas their customers buy holes!

Prospective purchasers might buy many 'things' rather than products as such, including advice, competitive superiority, consultancy, cost savings, diagnosis, peace of mind, performance, pleasure, productivity, profitability, problem analysis, quality, reliability, safety, satisfaction, security, self-confidence, service, speed of operation, solutions, technological advance – and many more.

2. *Why from you* – what is the buyer's perspective in choosing one brand rather than another?
As an example, the manufacturer of wire products little different from those of rivals featured in his advertising the complete service provided: analysis, competitive pricing, expert advice, laboratory facilities, product development, quality control, range, stocks, swift delivery, and after-sales service – all good reasons for buying 'me too' products from his company rather than competitors. 'Sourcing' of industrial products can be as important as brand image is for consumer products.

Other reasons for choosing one supplier rather than another, which could feature in your advertising, include availability, brand name, continuity, convenience, cost, credit terms, delivery, endorsements, familiarity, proof of performance, reliability, specification, suitability, value – and many more.

This second question leads logically to a third important consideration:

3. *Substantiation* – what *firm* evidence exists to justify your advertising claims? Communication models discussed in the next chapter stress the importance of 'conviction'. Never take it for granted that prospective purchasers will believe your product claims! Why should they?

You should also consider other decision criteria, by constructing a *purchasing profile*.

Purchase parameters

Another approach to creating persuasive messages is to review the parameters of a purchase.

When analysing any buying decision, construct a *purchasing profile*, selecting from a range of 'buy-scales'. These could include, not in any order of importance, the following:

Frequent	Infrequent
Regular	Irregular
Rational	Emotional
High involvement	Low involvement
Impulse purchase	Pre-planned
Brand loyal	Fickle
Voluntary	Involuntary
Constrained	Free choice
Individual decision	Consultative

Examples

A financial services example which illustrates the difference between the first two scales is home insurance, which involves a regular but infrequent decision. It is also a pre-planned, rational, high-involvement decision, usually taken by a single individual.

Having a pint of beer, on the other hand, would be a regular, frequent, low-involvement, emotional decision taken by a single individual on an impulse basis. Whether the drinker is brand loyal depends on the individual!

Purchase of a company-wide computer system implies an infrequent high-involvement consultative decision. The same parameters apply to buying replacement parts, which might also be a constrained decision, determined by the original purchase. Suppliers seeking to break the inertia of a repeat purchase cycle (resulting from existing stocks, service agreements and familiarity) might plan advertising which seeks a 'modified rebuy' as discussed in Appendix B. The original supplier will, of course, seek a 'straight rebuy'.

For some purchases such as repair of a broken window, the decision is an involuntary one taken for you by circumstances. Your task – aided by suitable advertisements – is to select a repairer. In this case you will actually seek out information: another example of how people use advertisements used to reach them.

This example also illustrates the need to consider both the long- and short-term effects of advertising, as well as consumers' entrenched beliefs (few, if any, in the case of a broken window) and short-term needs. Your immediate objective might be to attract possible customers who are in the market now but, at the same time, your advertising will also be seen by others who – although they have no current need – might want your product in future and, when the time comes, may recall your name as a possible supplier.

Another approach to buying decision analysis suggests that parameters, markets and motives change over time.

Innovation/diffusion

Readers are doubtless aware of the 'product life cycle' and its four stages: introduction, growth, maturity and decline. Innovation/diffusion analysis suggests that, over the cycle, potential purchasers differ both demographically and psychographically. They are accordingly categorized as:

a) Innovators.
b) Early adopters.
c) Late adopters.
d) Early majority.
e) Late majority.
f) Laggards.

Each category calls for different messages delivered through different media, according to your product's position on its life-cycle. A revolutionary new product in itself appeals to those who pride themselves on keeping abreast – if not ahead! – of whatever is new. Innovators are not only important in their own right, but also serve as 'multipliers' in spreading new technology. The word 'NEW!' will attract them just as surely as it puts off late adopters. Conversely, the 'Thousands of Satisfied Users' approach would re-assure Laggards as effectively as it was counter-productive for innovators.

The practical implications

Analysis of buying decisions, whichever approach is adopted, leads to different messages delivered through different media to different market groups at different times. Obvious, perhaps, but all too often overlooked.

Your next step

Having determined this need for individualized campaigns, the next step is to review how advertising communication actually works.

18 Models of communication

In the study of Man, it is easier to understand the species than the individual.

Francois, Duc de la Rochefoucauld

Two factors to consider when preparing effective advertising campaigns are the purchasing process just reviewed, and how communication can influence these decisions – the focus of this chapter.

Communication models

Alternative models seek to explain how the communication process works. There is no question of one model being right and the others wrong, but rather deciding which model applies to a given situation.

The better-known models include:

A I D A	Attention	Interest	Desire	Action
A C C A	Awareness	Comprehension	Conviction	Action
A T R	Awareness	Trial	Reinforcement	
Felt need	Search process	Evaluation	Purchase decision	Post-purchase feeling

AIDA

This formula suggests that the communication task is to attract *attention*, awaken *interest*, convert this into *desire*, and finally lead to *action*.

Often associated with consumer advertising, the model applies equally to business-to-business markets. At any one time only a few buyers may be actually interested in what is on offer. There are always potential customers but the problem lies in identifying them, especially when the possible purchase 'initiator' is hidden deep inside an organization, inaccessible to uninvited sales representatives. The advertising task under such circumstances is to persuade potential purchasers to identify themselves and request a demonstration. Advertisements should therefore provide sound reasons for positive action. The response then provides a list of prospects with an immediate or imminent product need. Advertisements which follow the AIDA formula, suggesting a course of action (e.g. telephone or return the coupon/reply card enclosed) can increase sales force productivity just as effectively as they sell consumer products.

Any market can be considered as a pyramid. At its apex are those few purchasers aware of their immediate need. Many more potential buyers are nearer the pyramid's base. Some may need the product – but not yet. Others should be in the pyramid, but are not yet aware of their need.

ACCA

An alternative heirarchy of effects therefore takes prospects through four levels of understanding. Prospects must first be made *aware* of a product and their need for it. This must be followed by *comprehension* of what the product can do to satisfy this need – a creative task which, for technical products, is by no means as simple as it sounds. The next stage is *conviction* – persuading prospects that the product actually does what is claimed. Text should anticipate possible sceptical reaction by providing credible information. It is not until the first three stages are completed satisfactorily that you can hope for *action*, and an actual purchase.

In some instances, particularly with revolutionary new products, the conviction stage presents a major obstacle. It may be necessary, if theoretical evidence is insufficient, to 'grip the nettle', install the new product without charge, and then adopt the testimonial approach – often extended by a series of case study advertisements, each describing a successful new application.

ATR

Another model recognizes the distinction between high and low involvement decisions and follows an *awareness – trial – reinforcement* heirarchy. Many decisions involve 'dissonance': any chosen alternative necessarily involves drawbacks, whilst rejected products have favourable features. In consequence those buying cars, as an example, will – after concluding the purchase – ask themselves 'Did I make the right choice?' Emphasis is therefore placed on reinforcement after the trial stage – particularly important when, as discussed earlier, existing users influence other potential purchasers.

Felt need

Felt need	*Search process*	*Evaluation*	*Purchase decision*	*Post-purchase feeling*

This model is best illustrated by the manufacturer of anti-corrosion chemicals whose advertising manager commented 'That's the one for us, but we're outside on the left.' His explanation was that if you actually need anti-corrosion chemicals, it is then too late as your machinery has already corroded! His advertising problem was thus to waken an unfelt need for *prevention*. The other steps in this model are discussed in Appendix B.

Other models

There are other approaches. One suggests a four-step model whereby the message must be:

Seen – Believed – Remembered – Acted upon

Yet another model analyses the communication role at the various stages of a six-step selling process:

Make contact – Arouse interest – Create preference –
Quote a price – Close the deal – Keep the customer happy

All models have one thing in common: they recognize the need to attract attention, without which existing and potential purchasers will not proceed to later stages of whichever heirarchy is selected.

Your next step

With a clear understanding of purchasing decisions and how communication works, you can now plan what to say and how to say it – in short, create arresting and persuasive advertisements.

19 What to say

I'll make him an offer he can't refuse.

Don Corleone, in Mario Puzo's *The Godfather*

All communication models depend on capturing attention, to lead prospects through their respective heirarchies of effects. Whatever attention device is selected, creative content must still arrest attention in its own right.

Contrary to popular opinion, capturing attention is *not* difficult. There are many easy ways to do so, including inserting your advertisement upside down. Alternatively, show a well-endowed but scantily-clad beauty or well-developed body-builder! Research may well show high recall of your upside-down advertisement, and favourable recall of eye-catching individuals – but minimal memory of product, brand, or benefits.

The same comment often applies to using celebrities as attention devices – the term 'video vampire' has been used to describe those instances in which viewers remember the celebrity but not the brand.

This can be equally true of radio commercials, where listeners remember well-known voices (or pairs of voices) rather than the product advertised. This problem is compounded when the same voices are used by a wide range of different advertisers, even to the point of over-exposure.

The difficulty lies not in attracting attention but in *keeping* it. Once this is recognized, the solution becomes easy – offer a benefit. Sometimes this promise is expressed in reverse: elimination of a negative such as a painful migraine headache.

Short pause to remind you of the 'constraints' aspect of situation analysis: the ASA's *Code of Advertising and Sales Promotion* imposes restrictions on health and medical products, and similar limitations apply in many countries.

Attracting and retaining attention depends on applying stringent creative discipline to the task of selecting – from the mass of information gathered earlier – the key concept on which to build advertising proposals.

Different practitioners adopt different approaches to deciding the copy platform. As always, there is no question of one being right and the others wrong, but rather of deciding which approach applies in particular circumstances.

USP

The *unique selling proposition* approach, developed by Rosser Reeves, suggests that:

> The consumer tends to remember just one thing from an advertisement – one strong claim or one strong concept. Each advertisement must make a proposition to the consumer. The proposition must be one that the competition either cannot or does not offer.

The implied rational or hard sell approach might be less effective, however, when there is little tangible difference between rival brands.

Brand image

For products very similar to each other (such as baked beans) David Ogilvy's *brand image* approach might be more suitable:

> It is the total personality of a brand rather than any trivial product difference which decides its ultimate position in the market.

This implies a more emotional approach with rich psychological overtones and non-verbal communications (including visual signals such as house style, non-product 'company' associations, and connotations of prestige and quality) which create a favourable brand image just as important as the message content, which backs up this image by a supporting rationalization

Positioning

Other practitioners refer to:

> The presentation of a product so that consumers distinguish it from competition in terms of satisfying an unfilled need. It is the product's basic selling idea to consumers.

As marketing becomes more competitive, it is increasingly important to consider your company's position from the customer's standpoint, in relation to consumer choice and the competition faced from rival suppliers.

Other approaches

Other creative approaches considered in the next chapter examine both what you say, and how you say it.

Series campaigns

Whichever creative approach is adopted, you must nevertheless decide whether the campaign should comprise one advertisement to be repeated, or a series of advertisements to appear in rotation.

Advertising must always be considered in continuity so that new campaigns build on and benefit from their predecessors. Any one campaign might, however, comprise a series of advertisements for one of two reasons:

1. Different messages

When products have a number of important attributes these may be featured in turn, in a linked series of advertisements, each cross-referring to the others, which appear in rotation.

As example, a leading credit card company featured in its advertising different aspects of its service – including the vast network of outlets accepting the card, its lost card replacement service, and insurance cover on goods purchased using the card. All were presented synergistically and linked by a common 'Does more than do you credit' theme.

2. Different expression

In this case there is no change in what is said, but it is expressed in different ways for the sake of variety. Much depends on your media schedule – high frequency could result in over-exposure of any one advertisement and, in extreme cases, could even be counter-productive.

The last paragraph could thus appear in the next chapter on 'How to say it' just as much under the present heading of 'What to say'.

Your next step

What to say concerns the *strategy* stage of advertising planning, whereby campaign objectives are converted into communication objectives – what must you say, for example, to persuade people to switch brands?

Whatever creative approach is adopted, the essential message could be expressed and then delivered in innumerable different ways – the creative and media tactics discussed in later chapters.

20 How to say it: text

Do you secretly feel you are inarticulate, but can never put it into words?

Boardroom graffiti

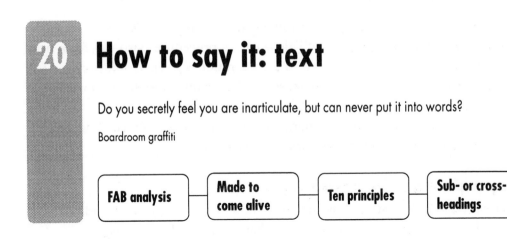

FAB analysis → Made to come alive → Ten principles → Sub- or cross-headings

The strategy of 'What you say' and the tactics of 'How you say it' are both important, but neither sufficient on their own. As mentioned in the last chapter, a number of creative approaches cover both aspects.

F A B analysis

This approach helps link what you say with how to say it, by distinguishing between features, advantages and benefits.

- The *feature* of a machine tool might be shorter setting-up time than competitors.
- The *advantage* is commencing production more swiftly.
- The *benefit* is increased production, which in turn leads to other benefits such as greater profit.

Advertisement text should be worded in such a way that features and benefits are directly linked.

A single-minded proposition made to come alive in a compelling way

The Saatchi & Saatchi creative approach stresses both aspects of communication. Strong message content is in itself not sufficient – if expressed in lacklustre fashion, it will fail to communicate. The agency philosophy thus concentrates on 'How you say it' just as much as 'What you say'.

Equally, making any advertisement come alive by inserting it upside down will not compensate for lack of a powerful message. (All rules can be broken on occasion. An audio-visual company's upside-down advertisement effectively drew attention to the dangers of faulty presentations. 'Relevant but unexpected' is another useful axiom – many advertisements, by saying exactly what everybody expects, fail to attract attention!) This agency's procedures also call for a firm decision on what to say before detailed consideration is given to how best to say it or which media should deliver the message. This emphasises the importance of creative planning.

Advertising agencies have no monopoly on developing creative philosophies. A leading consumer products manufacturer suggested:

Ten principles of good brand advertising

Like the Saatchi & Saatchi approach, these cover both what you say and how you say it. In essence, the ten principles state that good brand advertising:

1. Is consumer-orientated.
2. Concentrates on one selling idea.
3. Concentrates on the most important and persuasive idea available.
4. Presents a unique and competitive benefit.
5. Involves the consumer.
6. Is credible, sincere and true.
7. Is simple, clear, complete.
8. Clearly associates the selling idea with the brand idea.
9. Takes full advantage of the medium.
10. Demands action that will lead to the sale.

Supporting text relates each principle to consumer products – but the ten headings are equally applicable to business-to-business markets.

Sub-headings

Sub- or cross-headings serve several purposes – they can emphasise key copy points at the same time as they make an otherwise heavy layout visually more attractive. They also permit readers to 'self-edit' by skipping those sections not of interest, rather than simply stop reading. Advertisements which present unattractive 'walls of words' can be made digestible by use of sub-heads – this paragraph is thus equally relevant to the next chapter, which covers message presentation.

Your next step

This is to ensure that persuasive text is presented to best advantage.

How to say it: graphics

Insist on your right to be read.

Daniel L. Yadin, *Creating Effective Marketing Communications*

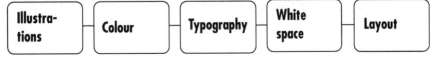

Whatever you say, the finished copy must be made to come alive. It is important, therefore, to think *visually*, so that the core concept can be reinforced by arresting illustrations and presentation. How you say it applies to graphics just as much as wording.

When fighting to capture and keep attention, it is equally important not to lose your own battle – many advertisements are cluttered, contain conflicting components, or are just plain boring!

The elements of design

Elements of design include visual presentation of the message's components – not only headline, text and sub-headings but also illustrations and other elements featured visually: brand symbol, coupon text, company logotype, and name and address.

Illustrations

The saying 'One picture is worth a thousand words' applies both to business-to-business and consumer products. Effective illustrations (rather than static pack shots) attract attention and can 'demonstrate' product benefits or – better still – show people actually benefiting. Types of illustration include numerous line and photo techniques, computer graphics and combinations thereof.

Colour

Illustrations – as well as headlines and body copy – can be strengthened by colour and, once again, alternative approaches are possible. The extra expense of full colour may well be worth while: perhaps to illustrate products and/or people as they really are, rather than in black and white. Although termed full colour, it is in fact achieved with only four standard process printing inks (cyan, magenta, yellow and black). An intermediate stage between single and full colour is second (or spot) colour: black plus red for example, used both to attract attention and emphasise parts of the message.

Typography

Typography can enhance – or destroy – your message. Appropriate typefaces increase legibility and present a distinctive image. Equally important is typographic layout – lines of excessive length are difficult to read, unless they are 'leaded' (with horizontal spacing between lines, which occupies valuable space, perhaps unnecessarily). An alternative approach is lines of shorter length, with text set in columns. Just as important is type size – many young so-called art directors ignore the fact that sight deteriorates with age, and persist in using small sizes despite the fact that older 'readers' cannot read them! Another common weakness is overlooking the importance of background – setting black text over dark colours (or reversing white text out of a pale background) detracts from legibility.

Sub-headings

The use of sub- or cross-heads to lighten an otherwise indigestible layout was discussed in the last chapter.

White space

Avoid the mistake made by many inexperienced executives whose attitude is 'I've paid £X for this space, so I'm not going to waste a single centimetre.' The outcome is an overcrowded layout, with no white space to place emphasis on headline and illustration, to balance the various components, and lead the eye logically through them.

Layout

The different components must be united harmoniously: there should be focus and impact, rather than disjointed elements in conflict. Layouts should, like text, have a logical sequence and follow, for example, the AIDA format – attracting attention through a benefit featured in headline and illustration, followed by text which converts interest into desire, leading to visual presentation of the action element. Layouts which follow this (or perhaps the ACCA or ATR) format are more effective than those which leave readers to find their own way through the maze.

Other media

Although expressed in print terms, message presentation is equally important for other media. Imagine a cinema or television commercial, for example, where:

1. Vision demonstrates Message A.
2. Voice-over delivers Message B.
3. Delivery too fast for comprehension.
4. Commentary conflicts with audio background.
5. Screen caption features Message C.
6. Caption obscures demonstration.
7. Demonstration detracts from caption.
8. Caption type so small as to be illegible.
9. Caption on screen too briefly to be read.
10. Caption lost on background – white on light, or black on dark.

Daniel Yadin's maxim – 'Insist on your right to be read' – applies equally to other media.

Cross-media campaigns

When writing and designing advertisements for multi-media campaigns, it is important to adopt a synergistic approach. This can be achieved by cross-media devices such as campaign slogans, colour, house style and typography. And, as has proved most effective, common sound effects on radio and television advertisements. When asked to recall a radio commercial for a well-known battery, many respondents described its physical appearance as shown on TV!

Your next step

Presenting your carefully polished message to maximum effect implies that you do have a message to present! But what if creative inspiration fails you? Where do you start? How best to overcome the tyranny of a blank sheet of paper? Turn to Chapter 22!

22 Sources of message content

Quickly, bring me a beaker of wine, so that I may wet my mind and say something clever.

Aristophanes

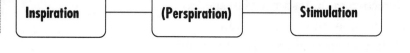

Inspiration — (Perspiration) — Stimulation

Selection of the correct benefit, brand image, copy platform, creative concept, key attribute, promise, single-minded proposition, or USP (depending on terminology) must depend on target market needs. Should inspiration fail you, creative thinking can be stimulated by review of earlier situation analysis, to provide a host of possibilities from which to choose.

Sources of creative ideas include:

- *Company characteristics:* Contemporary, big, expertise, helpful, facilities, technical resources.
- *Company heritage:* 'Established in the year XYZ', founders of the firm, the qualities of tradition, years of experience on which to call.
- *Comparison with competitors:* Product comparison, rather than 'knocking copy' – factual statements about why a product is better are more effective than those which denigrate rivals.
- *Disadvantages of non-use:* Resultant drawbacks, missed opportunities.
- *Newsworthiness:* New or improved, topical events, company anniversaries.
- *Product characteristics:* Availability or rarity, country of origin, disposable/refillable, performance in use.
- *How the product is made:* Raw materials, method of manufacture, quality control systems.
- *Price characteristics:* Credit terms, discounts, mark-ups, more for your money, lasts longer, trade margins, money off, cheaper – or more expensive.
- *Surprising facts:* About the product, users or usage.
- *User characteristics:* Experts use it, most firms use it.
- *Ways of using the product:* Particularly for multi-use products.

Additionally, there are active steps to take, including:

- Factory visits.
- Store checks.
- Product tests.
- Trial of competitors' products.
- Sell the product yourself.
- Analyse competitors' advertising.
- Brainstorming.
- Consumer discussion groups.
- And, above all, see for yourself: actually use the product!

Your next step

You are now ready to plan how best to deliver your carefully polished message. Unless, of course, you need foreign language versions for overseas media, as discussed in the next chapter.

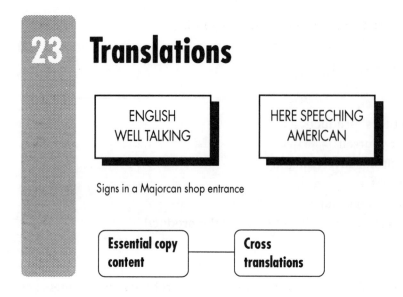

23 Translations

ENGLISH
WELL TALKING

HERE SPEECHING
AMERICAN

Signs in a Majorcan shop entrance

Essential copy content — **Cross translations**

There are a number of basic rules to observe if your advertisements are to appear in other countries.

Before all else, check that your product does in fact have a market, and that your brand name is acceptable. Continental products that would not do too well over here include:

Bum's biscuits – Sweden
Mukki yoghurt – Italy
Nora Knackers biscuits – Norway
Pschitt lemonade – France
Sor Bits mints – Denmark

Also, check local product usage habits, which could lead to different objectives, messages and media. Taking vodka as an example, in the UK this is largely a multi-use product (drunk with ice and various mixers) with sales peaking in summer. In the former Soviet Union, by way of contrast, vodka was primarily a single-use product (drunk neat as a specific against the cold) with a winter sales peak. Hence the current Russian advertising campaign promoting vodka as a multi-use product to be drunk with mixers, thereby ironing out fluctuations in the sales graph at the same time as increasing sales.

Assuming that your product would be welcomed if properly advertised, key considerations are:

1. *What to say*

Copy should be based on fundamental meanings, rather than literal translation of finely-polished copy (although technical text can be more word for word).

2. *How to say it – text*

Avoid figures of speech, which may be meaningless in other languages. 'Out of sight, out of mind' does not really mean 'Invisible idiot' as once translated! Those who overlook this warning may find themselves hoisted by their own petard. How many readers know what this means in English, let alone other languages? Anyone who *does* know should pat themselves on the back, put a feather in their cap, and then splice the mainbrace!

3. *How to say it – graphics*

Be wary of symbols, which may not be international, or even have different meaning in other countries.

Be equally careful of colours and illustrations, including backgrounds and the people in them.

Layout should allow for language differences. Preparing overseas material is a matter of length just as much as language – English text, when translated into Spanish for example, may require 25 per cent more space. This reinforces the importance of adequate white space in any layout.

When applied to audio-visual media such as cinema, television and video, the length problem is compounded by the fact that spoken dialogue may not match mouth movements.

For this reason, many international advertisers deliberately avoid 'Lip synch' copy where dialogue synchronizes with lip movements. They use instead 'Voice over' commentaries in as many languages as are necessary.

For even greater international applicability, some commercials rely entirely on music and sound effects, and dispense with both dialogue and captions.

As made clear above, it is of course essential that the visual content has a similarly world-wide applicability.

4. *Cross-translate*

Foreign language text should always be translated back into English, and – together with illustrations – checked against local customs, attitudes and literacy standards.

An example which illustrates the need for cross-checking is the launch advertisement for a perfume the brand name of which, in certain countries, symbolizes death and mourning. Furthermore 'The smell that won't go away' has a somewhat different meaning to 'Lingering perfume'!

Another example is the three linked 'Dirty face – Use our soap – Clean face' illustrations used on poster and press media. The advertiser alas overlooked the fact that the local language read from right to left!

Not the next step

Not the next step in the sense of my usual chapter-linking sentences, but too good to waste is the notice in an Austrian mountain hotel:

NOT TO PERAMBULATE THE CORRIDORS

DURING HOURS OF REPOSE

IN THE BOOTS OF ASCENSION

Your next step

With arresting and persuasive advertisements now ready, the next task is to plan a media schedule that delivers them to maximum effect.

PART 7:
Preparation of proposals – media

The only constant is change.

Karl Marx

Arresting and persuasive advertisements must be placed before prospective purchasers. This Part, which focuses how to do so as effectively and efficiently as
possible, covers:

24 The media available

Basic research is what I'm doing when I don't know what I am doing.

Werhner von Braun, pioneer space scientist

```
┌──────────────┐     ┌──────────────────┐     ┌──────────────┐
│ Media        │─────│ Do-it-yourself   │─────│ Candidate    │
│ differences  │     │ research         │     │ media        │
└──────────────┘     └──────────────────┘     └──────────────┘
```

The Preface explained that media would be treated generically, since they (and their audiences) differ between countries. Media costs and audience data are similarly omitted, since it is impracticable to quote local figures relevant to all readers on a world-wide basis. Furthermore, even if this were possible, current figures (like advertisements) date very swiftly.

To cover media properly on a world-wide basis calls for a separate book or rather a series of books: one per country.* However, if you are concerned with evaluating, planning and buying media in other countries, the basic questions are the same as for domestic media, discussed later. There are, however, important variations.

Media diversity and importance

Most (if not all) media exist in other countries, but their relative importance varies considerably. The UK is distinctive, for example, in its strong national press. In countries with larger geographic areas or wide cultural differences, the regional press is often more important.

The structure of television advertising, and its proportion of the total advertising expenditure, also varies. Those who visit other countries are often surprised by the frequency and amount of commercials, arising from differences in the time allowed. Seven minutes per hour (seven and a half in peak time) is the UK limit, whereas up to eleven minutes (or more) is permitted elsewhere. The UK norm is

---

*The innate modesty of any advertising man would normally prevent me from recommending the best book on UK media but, as I have no wish to upset my fellow author . . . *The Effective Use of Advertising Media* (5th Edition), Martyn P. Davis and David Zerdin, Century Business, ISBN 0 7126 7771 2.

under three minutes of commercials at any one time, whereas in other countries innumerable commercials are often screened consecutively.

Radio is more important in countries where economic pressures or illiteracy preclude purchase of other media. Listening habits may also differ, radio being almost a community activity. Cinema is similarly a more important medium in countries with open-air and drive-in screens, and where mobile cinemas travel between villages and are seen by the whole community.

Outdoor advertising often plays a more dominant role where controls over urban planning are not as strong as in the UK. Computer mapping systems facilitate poster planning in some countries, whereas in others competition between rival contractors (arising from lack of control) can be detrimental to outdoor campaigns. Poster facilities themselves vary, as some countries offer 'skyline' advertising – sites on the tops of buildings – unavailable here.

Quite apart from media differences, there may be differences in the way advertising is sold. Negotiation is a central part of the UK buying process, whereas in some countries laws may restrict discounting.

Finally it is important to recognize that advertising media are in constant flux – new media appear, and existing media adapt. Under such circumstances, half of any more detailed review would be out-of-date within a year, whilst the other half would not yet have happened. Anybody who wants proof of how fast the media change need only compare the five editions of my other book!

Resolve the problem

Never overlook your own expertise as a resident consumer of media, as distinct from a non-representative sample of one! Your own media habits are not necessarily those of the majority – but you have an invaluable working knowledge of local media, simply through living where you do. What is now necessary is to formalize that knowledge.

A first step is to systematize what you know, reviewing the operational aspects of each local media group:

1. *How is the medium structured, and into what categories does it subdivide?*
UK newspapers, as an example, can be categorized in various ways: national or regional, dailies or Sundays, broadsheet or tabloid, paid-for or free. Other media similarly sub-divide into distinctive categories.

2. *In what units is advertising bought or sold?*
Continuing the newspapers example, space is sold in the UK in single-column centimetres and multiples thereof. Insertions can be booked ROP as run-of-paper

(which permits the media owner to place the advertisement anywhere in the paper) or as special positions – perhaps front page, solus (without competition from other advertisers) or facing selected editorial.

Other media have their own individual selling units – 'pages' (and fractions thereof) for magazines and periodicals, 'sheets' for poster media (the terminology originating from the number of sheets of paper 'pasted' or posted on hoardings), and commercials of different lengths for television, cinema and radio.

3. *What are the medium's strengths and weaknesses?*
Since these vary country by country, local evaluation is the only answer, using the criteria discussed in the next chapter.

4. *What data sources are available, and what information is provided?*
This again varies country by country. The UK is fortunate in having a vast amount of media research data, the envy of most other countries. This however highlights both ends of the 'complaints' scale about research data – with some media, planners complain about lack of information whereas with others the complaint is that there is too much!

5. *What audiences are reached and, in turn, for what products and services are they suitable?*
The audience coverage data just discussed must be related to potential purchasers, again using the criteria discussed in the next chapter.

A functional study of this nature clarifies the mind, and paves the way for a different type of review.

Candidate media

This further analysis is best approached from the standpoint of 'candidate media' – a concept mentioned earlier – which indicates those meriting *detailed* study. You may consider, for example, that to reach the mass market you should use popular 'tabloids'. But to select between these newspapers, and use them in a way that makes the maximum contribution to your campaign objective, you must first study them *in depth*.

This investigation must go far beyond simple statistics (such as cost, circulation, readership and comparison of costs-per-thousand – all discussed in the next chapter) as different readers look at some pages more than others: this calls for in-depth analysis of both editorial content and advertising format.

What features does the publication carry on a regular basis, on which days of the week, and is adjacent advertising possible? The same advertisement could be made more effective by booking particular positions on specified feature pages which appear on certain days of the week in a given publication. Such positioning not only pin-points readers with interests relevant to your product, but also ensures that your message reaches them in a receptive frame of mind.

Gaining such in-depth media knowledge is no small task: it calls for daily study of every copy of each relevant medium – and its competitors – over many issues. Hence the importance of the candidate media concept, and having neither too long nor too short a list. Too long a list, and you will never complete your task. Too short a list, and you may overlook a medium which, through effective use, could made a positive contribution.

Whatever formal media surveys are available (discussed in the next chapter) never overlook 'Do-it-yourself' research. My own practice with overseas assignments is, on arrival, to sit down with my hosts and go through local media page by page, even if I do not speak the language. The outcome: I often know more about local media than those who live there. Having taken matters for granted, they are surprised at my 'expertise' – which they could easily have acquired themselves, simply by systematic study.

Your next step

Make an in-depth study of whatever candidate media you are likely to use. You will then be better able to evaluate them against more formal comparison criteria, discussed in the next chapter.

25 Media comparison criteria

The trouble with facts is that there are so many of them.

Samuel McCord Crowther

Quantitative criteria	Qualitative criteria	Usage and atti-tude studies	Cost

Throughout the world, a wide range of advertising media is available. On what basis should you choose between them? There is usually an equally wide range of research material to assist your choice. The fifth edition of my other book (see footnote on page 72) details more than thirty primary media surveys regularly published and lists numerous secondary sources, all giving invaluable data. Furthermore, there is a constant flow of new information. Other countries no doubt also have extensive sources.

Since it is impracticable to review all these many data sources, consider instead how they can assist you in selecting between media, and in planning effective media schedules.

It is first necessary to distinguish between quantitative and qualitative criteria. Quantitative refers to the numbers of copies sold or read, and viewers or listeners reached, while qualitative criteria concern subjective factors such as sound and movement, or high quality colour reproduction.

Quantitative criteria

All of relatively equal importance, these include:

- *Who?* Who will your advertising message reach, and how closely does this audience match the demographics of your target market?
- *Where?* A similar cross-checking of the medium's geographic (or geodemographic) coverage against target market location is again essential.
- *How many?* What is the total number, and how many in each area or demographic category? Much depends on definitions, discussed below.
- *Penetration?* What proportion of the total market does this number represent? It is unlikely that any one medium will give full market coverage – how best to reach the remaining proportion is discussed in Chapter 29.

- *Profile?* This differs from penetration in always adding up to 100 per cent. A magazine read by half the women in the country has 50 per cent penetration, but its profile is 100 per cent women. In practice, the profile might be 95 per cent women and 5 per cent men since even women's magazines have male readers. This over-simplifies since profiles may also be for age-bands, socio-economic groups, areas or product-usage categories. Whichever and however many sub-groups are detailed, profiles always total 100 per cent by definition.
- *Wastage?* Just as one single medium rarely achieves 100 per cent penetration, part of the audience delivered may not be in your market. Since rate-card cost is based on total coverage, you must assess what proportion constitutes less valuable contacts.
- *Additional data?* Although published reports contain many tabulations, the amount of information stored in computer data is much larger. There are usually facilities for obtaining (at an appropriate fee) additional tabulations: these can be provided by those commissioning the research, obtaining on-line access, purchasing your own copies of computer data, or specialist data-processing firms having access to the research.

There may be stages of answer to quantitative questions. With press media, for example, you often have readership as well as circulation figures (numbers of copies sold) – but much depends on definitions and research methods. To illustrate this point, contrast the data available about UK press and television audiences.

Television numbers may be quoted in terms of TVRs or Television Rating Points, with one TVR representing one per cent of the potential TV audience, which may be expressed in terms of homes or individuals. A viewer is defined as someone present in the room with a set switched on, for at least 15 consecutive seconds.

With press media the term 'reader' is equally important. Average issue readership (AIR) is defined as the number of people who claim to have read or looked at one or more copies of a publication for at least two minutes during its issue period (publication frequency).

Television's term 'in the room' covers anything from attentive watching to a casual glance while undertaking other activities. Similarly, the press 'read or looked at' term covers anything from thorough reading to a casual flip through, and it does not matter which issue – any issue will do.

Those readers consulting any media survey in other countries should check the document's 'Technical Appendix' for precise meanings of the coverage terminology. They should also check sample size and selection, and fieldwork, although discussion of these aspects of media research is beyond the province of this book.

When considering how many people your message reaches always remember that, while numbers are important, research methods are by no means perfect. This comment is not intended to find fault, but to set matters in context. It is also relevant that figures are necessarily dated in themselves: some surveys may be 6–12 months old before new data is published.

See also the note on *Mood* below, as *Positioning* can influence audience numbers as well as attitudes. Hence the importance of a thorough study of candidate media.

- *Cost?* This vital quantitative – and qualitative – criterion is discussed below.

Qualitative criteria

Not necessarily in order of importance, these include:

- *Delivery?* Do people read, listen to or watch your message, and how good is reproduction quality? In this respect, it is essential to keep abreast of how technological changes affect message delivery by the various media.
- *Mood?* What will be the audiences state of mind when they receive your message? This can be affected by positioning within media (booking special positions which preselect readers having relevant product interests) as much as by media choice.
- *When?* When will your message be delivered – this can be a matter of months, weeks or days (depending on when the medium is published) – and how does this relate to when you wish to stimulate your market?
- *Frequency?* How regularly can you contact potential purchasers? This again turns on when the medium is published.
- *Speed?* How quickly can the medium deliver your message? And how far in advance must you decide your advertising message? Technological changes have also had effect here, in that copy dates (even for full colour press advertisements) are shortening.
- *Flexibility?* Speed is not the only factor affecting flexibility. Direct mail is perhaps the ultimate example: as well as controlling when and how often you stimulate the market, you can also quantitatively 'turn the tap on or off' as needs dictate. You are also in full control of what you say and how you say it, and can even personalize messages.
- *Attention?* Brief attention is neither good nor bad until related to the communication task. Is your message brief enough for a ten-second commercial or poster, or must you convey price and product details?

- *Life?* Some magazines go on delivering your message until the journal falls to pieces, whereas radio delivers its impact at time of transmission. Much the same comment applies to television, but technological change is again important – see the reference to *Reliability* below.
- *Indirect influence?* Some media such as television have a marked impact on retailers, for example, thus helping secure wide distribution.
- *Availability?* What advertisement sizes and positions are on offer on the rate card, and in actual practice? If all the best positions are already sold, you may have to consider alternative media.
- *Constraints?* Some media owners impose restrictions on, for example, reversed white-on-black advertisements since these may cause printing problems. In other cases, legal or voluntary codes may classify certain products as unacceptable.
- *Reliability?* How certain are you that your message will appear, and can you rely on high quality delivery? Technological changes have improved message quality for most media, but not always their reliability. With television, for example, the vast majority of households now have remote control units and video-recorders. These facilities allow people to edit their viewing either by 'zapping' from one channel to another, or by 'zipping' fast forward on a video-recording, to avoid the commercials.
- *Weight of advertising?* How much advertising is carried, generally and for rival brands in particular? With media carrying vast amounts, your own advertisement may possibly be overlooked – hence the importance of attention devices, discussed earlier.
- *Facilities?* What will media owners do, in addition to delivering your message? Such facilities range from simple and free, to sophisticated services for which a fee (perhaps at cost) is charged. These could include help with creation and production of advertisements, additional computer runs of media data and help with scheduling, as well as back-up services such as telephone-answering and reply-handling facilities, sales force support, advance information to the trade of forthcoming consumer advertising, direct mail facilities, sales conference assistance, and market research services.
- *Cost?* This further consideration, discussed below, is both quantitative and qualitative.

Quantitative and qualitative studies

The difference between quantitative and qualitative criteria is essentially simple. Most relevant, however, is recent research which quantifies qualitative aspects through 'Usage and attitude studies' and measures, for example:

- *'Usage'* – regularity of reading, number of pick-ups, proportion read, time spent reading, etc.
- *'Attitudes'* – interesting/dull, most/least useful source of information, authoritative/unreliable, helpfulness of advertisements, etc.

Two rival publications might claim similar readership yet have very different U & A ratings – one offering a higher number of opportunities to see your advertisement, received in a far more favourable state of mind. There is little doubt which medium would deliver your message most effectively.

Cost

Colour costs more than black-and-white, and special positions or specified days of the week are charged at higher rates than run-of-paper or run-of-week insertions. Cost has therefore been left until last, not because it is unimportant – far from it! – but because it has both qualitative and quantitative connotations.

Cost varies not only with advertisement unit and attention device but also size of total order, since most media owners offer discounts for series bookings: the more insertions booked at one time, the larger the discount.

Other discounts relate to 'packages' of advertising. If you help media owners by being flexible in your requirements, they in turn help you by charging lower rates. If, however, you want complete control of exactly when your commercials are transmitted, which precise sites feature your posters, or which specified cinemas screen your commercial and in which weeks, you must pay the full price in the normal way. For cinema and poster media, such specific bookings are often termed 'line-by-line'.

These flexible packages are sometimes linked to the 'How many?' question, with media owners' charges being based directly on actual audience delivered, as revealed by research. GHI (Guaranteed Home Impressions) schemes, AGP (Audience Guarantee Plans) or TAP offers (Total Audience Packages) are examples of UK media applications as they apply to television, cinema and radio.

From time to time, most media owners extend other offers to boost sales in slack periods. These are many and varied but divide into two groups – a discount offer to sell the same amount of advertising at reduced charge, or alternatively a bonus offer of more advertising at no additional cost.

Cost and value for money

Cost is frequently considered together with quantity, and one medium compared with another, by what is termed CPT or 'cost per thousand' – the cost of reaching each thousand of the target audience. Usually expressed in pence, it is often used as a general measure of media cost and efficiency.

To calculate CPT, the cost of a publication's basic selling unit (in the UK, the single-column centimetres rate for newspapers or full-page costs for magazines, for example) is often divided by its circulation, in thousands.

Costs per thousand are frequently used in evaluating media, but this approach is alas often misused, being applied too loosely. To quote any cost per thousand figure is meaningless unless it is clear what is being measured. Before accepting the CPT for one medium in comparison with its rivals, ask a very basic question – *cost of what* per thousand *what?* For this reason, CPT calculations are frequently extended to particular advertisement units and attention devices in one publication rather than another. Equally, it may be calculated not for circulation but for readership, or for readership by a particular demographic group. Similarly, television costs per thousand may be calculated for specified audiences rather than numbers of sets switched on, and for different length commercials screened at different times.

Production costs

With some media, production costs (as distinct from media owners' charges) constitute only a small proportion of total costs, whereas for others they are sufficiently large to influence media planning.

The final choice

Clearly there is no such thing as the best medium. The benefits offered by various media must be contrasted with the needs of the advertising task. Any medium, or combination of media, could be best under certain circumstances, depending on objectives.

Your next step

With a sound knowledge of media and formal research data (supplemented by in-depth appreciation gained from do-it-yourself research) the next task is to plan a media schedule which delivers your message to maximum effect.

26 Overall planning

Drowning problems in an ocean of information is not the same as solving them.

Professor Ray E. Brown

```
┌─────────────┐     ┌─────────────┐
│ Case-rate   │─────│ Media       │
│ spending    │     │ allocations │
└─────────────┘     └─────────────┘
```

To the three planning stages of situation analysis, objective and budget must now be added creative requirements: the joint decision on advertisement unit and attention device discussed earlier.

Two other important considerations (in addition to research data and in-depth knowledge of candidate media) affect the media planning process.

1. Market weighting and case-rate spending

Situation analysis established earlier that 'frequency and value of purchase, and geographic location . . . influence both messages and media'. Irrespective of whatever media are used, these underlying considerations influence where and when to target advertising money.

Media planners often adopt 'case-rate' spending (the name derives from the number of cases of your product sold) allocating money according to market weights or values – which could be by area, market segments, month, or indeed product. If a given area accounts for 30 per cent of sales, it seems logical to spend 30 per cent on media which stimulate that area. Similarly, if 20 per cent of sales occur in a given month, 20 per cent of media expenditure targets that same month. The same logic applies to market segments, and to expenditure by product. Case-rate calculations frequently allow for a number of factors simultaneously, so that a suitable proportion of the budget is allocated to a particular product, expenditure on which is then divided among target groups according to their levels of expenditure. These sums are then further allocated to individual sales areas, and then month by month within these areas, in accordance with sales figures.

Hence the importance of thorough situation analysis, to provide media planners with statistical information as to product sales by month and area, and purchasing figures by market segment: all essential data if the advertising budget is to be targeted accordingly.

The principle behind case-rate spending is simply to spend money when and where sales figures indicate it should be spent. High sales call for high expenditure to maximize benefit from this potential, whereas less money is allocated to those products, market segments, areas and times of year where sales figures indicate the market has little propensity to buy.

Although planners may later challenge the underlying assumption of case-rate spending (see Chapter 28) the method nevertheless provides a sound initial basis for schedules which directly link media expenditure to marketing data.

2. Media allocations

A parallel aspect of general planning involves allocating money to different media groups such as press or television – a decision sometimes termed the *media split*.

Funds are provisionally allocated on an inter-media basis – so much for television, so much for press, and so much for other media – and preliminary schedules then costed for each media group. All going well, initial allocations will be sufficient to finance effective schedules in all desired media.

Conversely, these preliminary costings may reveal that the television allocation, for example, is insufficient. If the sum allocated to press leaves some latitude, however, the media split will be adjusted accordingly, with funds transferred from one allocation to another. The ideal media split is rarely achieved at first attempt.

Your next step

Since final media allocations depend on agreed preliminary costings for each media group, attention now turns to the variables on which these costings depend.

27 Media scheduling: the basic variables

Facts that are not frankly faced have a habit of stabbing us in the back.

Sir Harold Bowden

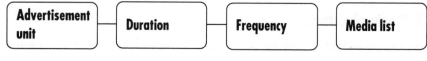

Before planning how to spend each allocation, it is wise to recall an unwelcome home truth – there is never enough money! In consequence, media scheduling necessarily involves – as with deciding the media split – constructing and costing alternatives, and then reviewing them to select the best.

The basic variables

With advertisement unit (and attention device) agreed, media planners can now consider how best to spend the sum allocated to each media group. A first step is to relate, in expenditure terms, the agreed planning unit, campaign duration, how frequently advertisements should appear, and in which media. The four basic variables are thus:

- Advertisement unit.
- Duration.
- Frequency.
- Media list.

Most preliminary costings will, more often than not, indicate over-spending – rarely the other way round, alas! It is always possible to ask for more money, but this is seldom wise as the budget was decided only after careful consideration.

It is equally possible to return to the media split, and transfer spare funds from one allocation to another, but what if *all* are over budget?

Another possible solution is to reconsider the four basic variables, but three have implications extending beyond media.

Creative staff are now hard at work on the basis agreed. Any move to cut back the advertisement unit or attention device will be most unwelcome and could perhaps damage the campaign, quite apart from the waste of time, effort and money that scrapping their proposals would involve.

Two other basic variables – frequency and duration – also have wider implications. Marketing staff will mistrust any campaign proposal that gives too infrequent a stimulus or leaves the market uncovered for any significant period of time.

The only basic variable media planners can adjust independently is the media list – must advertisements indeed appear within publications A, B, C and D? If planners are, however, convinced that all four titles (or media groups) are essential to achieve full market coverage, it appears that the planning process is at an impasse. However . . .

Your next step

. . . there are other possibilities.

28 Other variables

It is more important to select one of half-a-dozen possible plans and get on with the job than it is to prolong the debate until the last shred of doubt as to which is the perfect best can be removed.

Clarence R. Randall

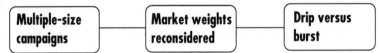

| Multiple-size campaigns | Market weights reconsidered | Drip versus burst |

To avoid an over-spending impasse, consider three other scheduling possibilities:

1. Multiple-size campaigns

When financial limitations do not permit regular half pages every week for example, campaigns are sometimes based on two sizes – a half-page advertisement followed by three consecutive quarter-pages, in a monthly repeating pattern. On occasion a third size, perhaps a full-page launch advertisement, might be used – primarily to impress the trade and to help representatives 'sell in' to retailers.

Multiple-size campaigns give the best of both worlds: impact and repetition. The same principle applies to other media, with TV campaigns featuring different length commercials. If well executed, viewers seeing a shorter version will recall the longer commercial! Exploring this solution when creative work is at execution stage is unnecessarily expensive, so ideally this possibility would be considered earlier, when reaching initial creative/media agreement.

2. Market weights reconsidered

Case-rate spending, whereby media expenditure matches sales figures, might be chicken-and-egg – the reason target group A or area B or month C accounts for only 10 per cent of sales is that it receives only 10 per cent of the total stimulus. Together with marketing staff, media planners therefore review matters in terms of potential rather than actual sales.

One alternative is to increase expenditure beyond that suggested by case-rate figures. If sales in a particular area were elastic, spending more money could be a wise investment, in that additional expenditure will pay for itself in terms of increased sales. You may rightly think that this makes matters worse rather than better: *We're already overspent, and here we are spending even more money!* Where are the additional funds to come from?

The alternative to spending more is of course to spend less. If demand in certain market segments or areas or months is inelastic then, even if media expenditure were reduced, sales will remain stable. This could be for either negative or positive reasons.

One target group may simply have no spare cash at certain times of year, so there is little point in trying to persuade them to buy more. There may, however, be a minimum expenditure level they have little choice but to maintain, even if advertising stimulus were reduced. On a positive note, some customers may be more brand-loyal than others, with less call to remind them as frequently. A minimum level of reminder advertising is necessary for both groups, but the frequency of stimulus – and thus the level of expenditure – can be reduced in the belief that demand levels are inelastic.

3. Drip versus burst

A drip campaign comprises regular advertising, in the belief that 'constant dripping wears away a stone'. Advocates of the burst approach, however, argue that some drip advertisements are too small to be noticed, and that increased impact would be more effective.

Burst campaigns achieve this by a combination of both multiple-size and increased/decreased expenditure approaches, the difference being that one multiple-size is zero! Advertising is cut back in certain weeks to boost impact in others, with periods of no market stimulus alternating with bursts of heavy advertising.

On occasion, such campaigns are planned on a media group basis. Alternating periods of burst advertising and zero activity in one medium are planned to interlock with converse periods of zero activity and burst advertising in another. This gives the target market continuity of advertising stimulus, but from alternating sources for variety.

Your next step

This is to review the alternative schedule possibilities in terms of their practical effects – how often and how many times will each target group see your advertisements?

29 Multi-media campaigns

> When we reach the sphere of mathematics we are among processes which seem to some the most inhuman of all human activities and the most remote from poetry. Yet it is here that the artist has fullest scope for his imagination.
>
> Havelock Ellis

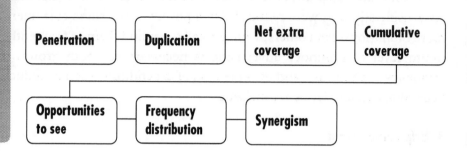

Penetration

Few if any advertising schedules depend on a single medium – to achieve full market coverage most campaigns feature two or more. One candidate medium may cover a major proportion of your market, and (as explained earlier) a penetration figure of 50 per cent means in simple terms that half your potential customers have an opportunity to see your campaign. How best to reach the other half?

Duplication versus net extra coverage

Two further candidate media may be considered but, if the readership of one overlaps that of the primary medium this duplication means that, rather than reach new prospects, you have unknowingly changed one of the four basic variables: frequency. Readers seeing both publications have two opportunities (rather than one) to see your advertisements and, in such circumstances, you would seek an alternative medium that provides net extra coverage, with minimum duplication.

Cumulative coverage

The two publications together give a cumulative coverage figure. Should this still represent insufficient market penetration, the solution is to seek additional media providing ever more net extra coverage, thus taking cumulative coverage even higher. This 'building bricks' approach may continue until budget restraints indicate it is uneconomic to cover the small proportion of potential purchasers not yet reached. Economists refer to 'The Law of Diminishing Returns', and the same law applies to media scheduling.

Frequency distribution

To illustrate the practical outcome of this overlap process as simply as possible, consider a campaign based on two publications, X and Y, with title Y providing a significant element of next extra coverage but, at the same time, some duplicated readership. Those who read only title X have one opportunity-to-see your advertisement (OTS) and the same argument applies to those who read only publication Y. Those who read both publications clearly have two opportunities-to-see. Most campaigns call for significantly more insertions, and frequency distribution summarizes the number of opportunities each different target group has to see your advertisements. This should of course reflect desired frequencies and actual (or potential) market weightings.

The same principle applies to other media such as television and radio where you would be equally interested in cumulative coverage and opportunities-to-see (or hear). Television audiences are usually measured by 'ratings' and a TV rating of 33 per cent simply means that one-third of the potential audience had opportunity to see your commercial. Pause for a moment to consider the extreme outcomes of three transmissions each achieving a 33 per cent rating.

One possibility is that the commercial was seen three times by the same third of the total TV audience – call them Group A. At the other end of the scale, the commercials were screened to different thirds in turn – call them Groups A, B and C – thus cumulatively covering 99 per cent of the total potential audience, all of whom had one opportunity-to-see. Part-way between these two extremes Group A could have one opportunity-to-see, whereas Group B had two opportunities, at the expense of Group C to which no opportunity was presented.

In summary, the possibilities are as shown on page 90.

This theoretical illustration is of course an over-simplification as television schedules are in practice far more complicated, with most campaigns comprising numerous transmissions spread over many weeks. It nevertheless indicates how alternative ways of scheduling the same number of transmissions (or insertions) can achieve very different results in terms of the proportion of potential purchasers reached, and the number of opportunities different target groups might have to see your advertisement.

None of the three possibilities illustrated is better than the other two. All turns on your specific objective, and whether this was:

- to reach all prospects, even if with only one insertion?
- to reach one (or more) market segments more frequently than others?

Any possibility could be best, depending on your objective.

Synergism

Cumulative coverage and frequency distribution apply across media groups as well as individual publications – using one medium to supplement (or rectify any weaknesses in) the coverage of another. Here the concept of 'synergism' becomes important. One media planner explained this as making two plus two add up to five rather than four! All media overlap in that people read newspapers and magazines, watch TV, listen to the radio, and see posters. Some media groupings are more synergistic than others, however, as when people hearing a radio commercial recreate in their mind's eye the visual aspects of a parallel TV campaign. With other media groupings, by way of contrast, creative and media must work far harder to achieve synergism.

Your next step

With alternative media schedules calculated and costed, the next step is to evaluate them to select the best.

Illustration of alternative TV scheduling options

Group reached	Cumulative coverage	Frequency distribution
A + A + A (Duplication)	33%	A = 33% × 3 OTS B = 33% × 0 OTS C = 33% × 0 OTS
A + B + C (Net extra coverage)	99%	A = 33% × 1 OTS B = 33% × 1 OTS C = 33% × 1 OTS
A + B + B (Overlap)	66%	A = 33% × 1 OTS B = 33% × 2 OTS C = 33% × 0 OTS

30 The final schedule

I cannot give you a formula for success, but I can give you the formula for failure: try to please everybody.

Herbert Bayard Swope

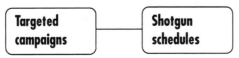

Numerous options are open to the media planner. All must be explored, different schedules developed, and the best selected. Effective media schedules are rarely (if ever) achieved at first attempt but only after costing and comparing many alternatives.

As there is never enough money, all media schedules necessarily represent a compromise. Planners must therefore decide which is the more important: impact, frequency, campaign duration or the range of media? Increases in one variable can be achieved only at the expense of others.

Targeted campaigns

While some element of compromise is inherent in any advertising campaign, it is important to avoid a weak schedule. Any media planner who falls into the trap of trying to please everybody by meeting all requests will end up with an ineffective schedule which delivers small infrequent advertisements spread over too wide a range of media.

One established media planning axiom is 'Concentration-Domination-Repetition' which results in targeted campaigns concentrated in a limited number of media in such a way that advertisements have impact, and appear regularly throughout the campaign period.

The shotgun principle

The very opposite media planning approach is the shotgun principle mentioned earlier, often adopted by advertisers launching new products into unknown markets. The same approach can be applied by those whose fragmented markets cannot be defined in terms of conventional demographic data. How can you deliver messages to widely diffused markets when there may be no medium or group of media which cover these target groups? Consider, as examples, the problem of trying to target people prone to back-ache, or businesses needing a portable office building on a short-term basis.

If 'Concentration-Domination-Repetition' is not possible, the alternative is to pepper the market on the shotgun principle. Such campaigns often comprise a wide spread of small direct-response advertisements which, through their headlines, select potential purchasers from the total audience reached.

As already explained, shotgun schedules can also serve as a market research tool. In such cases, the campaign is executed on a flexible basis, according to results. Depending on these results, it may then be possible to plan a full-scale targeted campaign. In such cases the five 'separate' planning stages – situation analysis, setting objectives, preparation of proposals, execution, and evaluation – are directly interlinked.

Your next step

With proposals for advertising messages and media prepared, your next step is to consider communicating with your target groups through the full range of promotional media. These alternative messages and media are reviewed in the next Part.

PART 8:
Alternative messages and media

Have regard for your name, since it will remain with you longer than a great store of gold.

The Apocrypha, Ecclesiasticus 41:12

This book concentrates on *advertising,* defined earlier as 'the use of paid-for media space or time'. If your campaign is to achieve maximum results, however, it should be supplemented by, and synergistic with, other forms of promotion. As these demand far more attention than can be given in a book devoted to advertising, the purpose of this Part is simply to alert you to their importance.

Chapter 31 therefore covers:

- The editorial route.
- Created media.
- Other message sources.

31 Alternative communications

White man talk with forked tongue.

Hollywood westerns 'Redskin' folklore

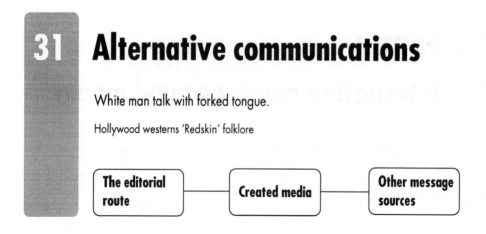

| The editorial route | — | Created media | — | Other message sources |

Chapter 1 established the functional advantages of advertising, which justify the expenditure involved. This does not mean, however, that other messages and media do not have a positive part to play – nor that you can overlook the danger of inadvertently talking with forked tongue!

The editorial route

Advertising is not the reason why most media exist, but a means of helping them to do so. Newspapers and magazines are read for editorial, and television watched for news and entertainment. Radio audiences, too, tune in for news and entertainment. Never forget that your *new* product is 'news' and could feature in editorial just as much as advertising. Hence the need for effective media relations and an active programme of news releases, press conferences and editorial features.

Created media

Although numerous media can serve to contact your target market, through both advertising and editorial, you may find that even this wide range does not fully meet your communication needs, and you must therefore create new media.

There is literally no limit to the range of created media, which could include:

- Advisory bureaux.
- Annual reports.
- Audio-visual devices.
- Awards and prizes.
- Competitions.
- Conferences.
- Demonstrations.
- Display material.
- Facility visits.
- Films.
- Incentives.
- In-house exhibitions.

- Gifts.
- House journals.
- Newsletters.
- Open days.
- Presentations.
- Printed material.

- Provision of equipment.
- Provision of services.
- Samples.
- Seminars.
- Speakers' panels.
- Videos.

Those already converted to *The Alternatives Approach* might consider their reason for creating media. Is it for merchandising purposes, to push products towards people? Alternatively is it for sales promotion reasons, to pull people towards products? The created media listed can be used to achieve either purpose. Hence the need, as with advertising planning, to specify a clear and precise objective.

The paradox of created media is that, as well as creating the medium, you must also create an audience for it. This raises matters in illogical order, however, since nobody should ever create a medium without first having a specific target audience in mind. Equally, you must decide in advance how to deliver the created medium to this created target market. Booklets, leaflets or videos – however well created – cannot deliver their message from a cupboard! Contrast this with advertising and editorial, when you know from readership, viewership or listenership data precisely who you will reach, and how your message will reach them.

A further point is that those who create media become media owners in their own right. Many house journals are subsidized by the sale of advertising space. Other companies' created media may present both advertising and editorial opportunities, while your own may present opportunities to others.

Other message sources

Consider also the concept of message sources, and how existing and potential customers receive information about your organization and its products. Those involved in marketing planning often categorize their activities under the headlines of 'the four p's' – *product, price, place* and *promotion.*

This review has so far considered only promotion, but the other three p's have equally important implications.

Your product (or service) itself delivers a message through its name, design, packaging and presentation.

Price also has marketing communications implications – lower price does not necessarily result in increased sales. Prospective purchasers often equate price with quality, and may suspect that low prices mean cheap and unreliable merchandise rather than price-advantageous products. Earlier discussion of messages covered the concept of positioning and many campaigns are based on this – low price being justified by 'The Price Promise', whereas costly products are promoted as 'Reassuringly expensive' or even 'The Most Expensive!'

Place is important too – consider products widely available through any outlet irrespective of facilities and expertise and – by way of contrast – merchandise available only direct or from dealers selected for their expert advice and after-sales service.

Promotional planning

Promotional planning should (within the constraints of the budget) encompass communicating through the full range of media – editorial as well as advertising and, if necessary, creating additional media – against the background of the other three p's and indeed all target market message sources.

The need to co-ordinate these other communications and avoid disparate 'forked tongue' messages is discussed in Chapter 32, which covers campaign approval.

Your next step

With proposals for arresting and persuasive advertising messages delivered by effective and efficient media plans, supplemented by other communications, your next task is to review these proposals to ensure that they are the best possible.

PART 9: Approval of proposals

I'm like an orchestra conductor. I don't write the music. I just make sure it comes out right.

Christopher Kraft

If preparing proposals in-house, you have doubtless considered various messages and media.

Alternatively, if using external services, the advertising agency has probably submitted just one proposal for approval.

By what criteria should you select from your own alternatives, or approve the agency's proposal?

This Part therefore covers:

Chapter 32 – Mistakes to avoid
Chapter 33 – The correct criteria.

32 Mistakes to avoid

Refusing to have an opinion is a way of having one, isn't it?

Luigi Pirandello

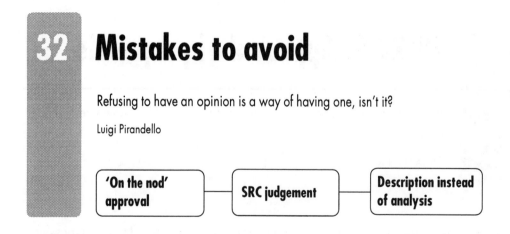

'On the nod' approval — SRC judgement — Description instead of analysis

The common mistakes to avoid when assessing proposals are best illustrated by a three-part practical exercise I set to open advertising seminars:

1. Delegates select, from a supply of newspapers and magazines, two advertisements – one good and one bad, but without indicating which is which. These are pinned up in random order, and numbered.
2. Delegates then write and submit for subsequent analysis brief critiques of their selection: 'I chose advertisement X which I think is good because . . . , and advertisement Y which is bad because . . .'
3. The final part of the exercise is for delegates to complete an 'Evaluation sheet' rating each advertisement as good, so-so (if they are uncertain) or bad.

I then calculate and distribute scores for each advertisement, based on ratings given. The outcome, to varying degrees, is always much the same.

The first mistake – approval 'on the nod'

There are always a large number of so-called so-so scores, but there is in fact no such thing as a so-so advertisement! A campaign may have little effect on the target market, but advertisers should have better uses for money! Approving a proposal 'on the nod' – perhaps because 'The agency should know what they're doing' is no way to ensure a successful campaign. The moral is that, if you are uncertain (or if the agency cannot convince you) you should withhold approval. The 'clincher' to this argument is that the so-so advertisements on display probably cost more than the group's combined salaries – and that's for one insertion! Over the year?

The second mistake – personal opinions

There are few (if any) advertisements which delegates are unanimous in agreeing are either good or bad. Putting this another way, for each advertisement one delegate rates good, there's someone at the seminar who thinks it's bad. Conversely, for each advertisement they think bad, there is somebody there who rates it good. The reason: delegates are expressing personal opinions – or, more technically, are using *self-reference criteria* (SRC). To evaluate any proposal properly, you must view it from the target market standpoint. If I am to evaluate an advertisement aimed at pregnant women then – with some difficulty! – I must imagine myself a pregnant woman! On occasion, it may be impossible to make such an evaluation – in which case market research is essential. But beware of those instances when you mistakenly think you can make a proper evaluation, whereas in reality this is just not possible. Research into TV commercials aimed at children proved this very point – advertisements adults liked were hated by the children, whilst those which appealed to children were disliked by the parents. Many advertisements or creative concepts are pre-tested for this very reason.

The third mistake – descriptive evaluation

To conclude the seminars I tape to each advertisement the relevant critique, which delegates evaluate at the same time as rescoring the advertisements. They swiftly appreciate that the critiques are largely *descriptive* – yet there is little need to describe what people can see for themselves: too much or too little copy, eye-catching or unattractive illustrations, over-crowded or illogical layouts, illegible typography or poor quality reproduction. What is needed is *analytical* evaluation, using proper criteria.

In passing, the reason for using press media is simply that it makes the exercise operationally easier, with no need for the fast-forward and rewind involved in discussing television, cinema or radio commercials. The same analytical process should apply, however, to all media.

Your next step

Avoid the three classic errors, and use instead the proper criteria described in the next chapter – just as delegates do when re-scoring their advertisements at the close of the seminar. The outcome: very different ratings!

33 | The correct criteria

Experience is what enables you to recognize a mistake when you make it again.

Earl Wilson

```
Prosaic ——— Creative
aspects        aspects
```

Approving proposals is a task everybody thinks they can do – show an advertisement to a layman, and he can always suggest improvements! Even experienced executives fail to 'think back' from the proposals in front of them, to check if they integrate with marketing objectives.

Checking can be considered under two headlines – prosaic and creative aspects. All too often, in their eagerness to discuss the creative, many managers overlook the duller aspects which, if not as they should be, can fatally undermine advertising effectiveness. Since these concern the campaign's very basis, they are considered first.

The prosaic aspects

Three important considerations must be investigated.

1. Changes
What changes have taken place since original briefing? With major changes planning should return to situation analysis stage, but what about minor changes? In your own interests, make this check. Failure to do so could result in disappointed customers as well as reprimands for featuring, as examples, out-of-date prices or product details, and old addresses or telephone numbers.

2. Marketing interlock
The consumer advertising campaign should interlock with parallel efforts to secure wide product availability, a task in which direct mail and the trade press can make a significant contribution. If your product is not in fact available when the campaign breaks, your advertising could increase *competitors'* sales rather than your own since retailers or distributors, rather than lose their profit, could recommend rival brands.

For companies which market their products direct, on the other hand, the marketing interlock might call for a steady flow of sales leads.

3. Constraints

Messages should of course be prepared in accordance with the legal and voluntary controls investigated at situation analysis stage. As these codes change from time to time, however, it is advisable to re-check before implementing the campaign. Indeed, some media control systems specify that proposals must receive official approval before execution.

The creative aspects

With less interesting aspects satisfactorily checked, attention can now focus on messages and media. Before considering the detailed proposals, however, remind yourself of the answers to two fundamental questions.

1. What is the specific advertising strategy?

Campaign objectives affect both messages and media. As earlier discussion made clear, there is little point in hoping that advertising will increase sales – where are these additional sales to come from? A good advertisement clearly reflects how it seeks to achieve this increase – persuading people to switch brands, bringing new purchasers into the market, or getting existing users to use more. Alternatively, it should reflect some other campaign objective discussed earlier, which would call for equally specific messages and media.

2. What core message has been selected?

Depending on terminology, which benefit, copy platform, brand image, creative concept, key attribute, promise, or unique selling proposition will trigger customer response? A good advertisement clearly reflects the potential purchasers' psychology and buying motives. Creative work is vital for effective advertising, but you must avoid seeking creativity for its own sake. When approving proposals, beware of advertisements which sell creative gimmicks rather than products.

With answers to these two vital questions clearly established, you can now examine the actual proposals, to assess them in the light of two further considerations.

3. How effectively will your elected appeal be delivered?

This in turn breaks down into separate checking operations – messages and media.

a) *Messages* Does the advertisement attract and retain attention? Has the single-minded proposition been made to come alive in a compelling and memorable way? How effectively does the illustration convey the selected appeal? Is it backed up by equally persuasive text, attractively and legibly presented? Will the message be delivered to maximum advantage as regards printing or transmission quality?

My favourite office notice (one of a series of mailings by Brian Holland & Partners) declares:

> # The strongest drive is not sex or greed. It is one person's need to ~~change~~ another's copy.

Not that polishing the text is unimportant – far from it – but this is a pointless exercise if the first two questions have not been answered satisfactorily. Perhaps you should hang this notice on your office wall, as defence against self-appointed advertising experts seeking to rewrite your copy?

b) *Media* Earlier chapters on media planning outlined the two-stage process – construction of alternative schedules followed by evaluation to select the best, so there is no need to describe this process again.

   As with discussion of message approval, all that is necessary here is to set this checking operation in the context of both preceding questions. Only after these are answered satisfactorily is it worth checking the media schedule's efficiency.

4. *Are the proposals comprehensive, cohesive and continuous?*

This question also sub-divides:

a) *Comprehensive* If advertising is to make its maximum contribution, it should be supplemented by other communications – the editorial route, created media, and all target market message sources.

b) *Cohesive* Campaign components must interlock. Your efforts will be ineffective if advertising delivers Message A, public relations Message B, while created media deliver Message C. Under such circumstances, any target market would be confused. Rather than fragmented efforts, you should strive for synergism whereby separate components reinforce each other, thereby multiplying the media effect.

c) *Continuous* Promotional efforts should also be comprehensive and cohesive over time, so that all new proposals build on and benefit from earlier campaigns.

Your next step

Once sure that proposals in their final form will make maximum contribution to campaign objective, your next step is to put them into effect.

Alternatively, your task may be to seek Board approval. In which case you should present campaign proposals using the same criteria – and perhaps have your 'The strongest drive . . . ' notice in reserve!

PART 10: Execution of proposals

It always seems to me that I am doing more work than I should do. It is not that I object to work, mind you: it fascinates me, I can sit and look at it for hours. I love to keep it by me; the idea of getting rid of it nearly breaks my heart.

Jerome K. Jerome, *Three Men in a Boat*

Like approval of proposals, their execution can be considered from two standpoints – prosaic and interesting. Both feature in the following chapters:

34 Implementing proposals

The secret of success in life is for a man to be ready for his opportunity when it comes.

Benjamin Disraeli, onetime British Prime Minister

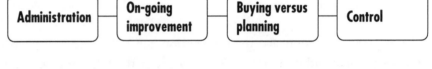

The preamble explained that, as with approval of proposals, their execution involves both interesting and prosaic aspects. Within this chapter, interesting aspects are sandwiched between the dull – this does not mean, however, that you can overlook the latter, if your proposals are to be executed to maximum effect.

Administration

Your plan exists only on paper. Implementing it entails a vast amount of detailed work – individual orders must be sent to all media on the schedule, and creative proposals converted into actual advertisements. The necessary administrative and production work is a major operation that should not be overlooked. Furthermore, this is an area where mistakes not only cost money but can undermine campaign effectiveness. Added to which, media owners' deadlines leave little room for error. 'Check everything, and then double-check' is perhaps the only safe solution.

On-going improvement

Execution should not be simply 'carrying out orders' but approached as a positive process. Television advertising is the extreme example, as schedules are usually planned in outline only, before future programming is known. Transmission times for most TV commercials are shifted repeatedly as the latest viewing figures are released or new programmes announced. With other media alterations are less frequent but rate changes, new circulation or readership figures, the launch of a new magazine or newspaper, or the closure of an existing title, all mean that schedules must be reviewed in the light of new circumstances, and changed accordingly. It is true to say that if a media schedule is executed exactly as originally planned, someone must be asleep on the job.

Furthermore, tactical advantage can be now be taken of last-minute offers by media owners. Advertisers known to have contingency reserves set aside for this very purpose (and who take swift decisions) find many advantageous offers come their way!

Buying versus planning

Positive implementation can also bring financial benefits. A buyer with expert knowledge of the media market place can make a valuable contribution to the budget by negotiating special deals: buying premium positions at standard rates or securing valuable discounts on normal rate card costs.

As discussed earlier, some practitioners use this route to build a contingency reserve, rather than set aside a given sum in advance. They too are well placed to snap up bargains!

Some practitioners separate planning and buying, believing that the abilities called for in implementing campaigns differ markedly from those needed at planning stage which, by comparison, seems a dull arithmetical exercise.

Control

While executing and improving your media schedule, keep expenditure under tight financial control. Running totals of expenditure month by month against schedule, by media-split allocations, together with incursions into (and availability of) contingency reserves, and savings achieved by expert buying, all combine to form a vital tool of control.

Your next step

Before moving to the next formal stage in the planning process, evaluation of results, it is wise to double-check that others are geared up to cope with the response your advertising will stimulate.

35 Follow-through

Advertising can bring the customer in only once: repeat business depends on the quality of the service.

John Petersen of The Petersen Partnership, when Group Marketing Director of Trusthouse Forte

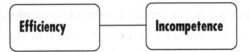

Efficiency — Incompetence

In an ideal world, this chapter would be superfluous! If a company invests time, effort and money to stimulate the market, it should surely cope swiftly with the response generated.

In practice, however, advertising is not always integrated with other activities. In too many cases, managers who took 'follow-through' for granted learned later of unacceptable delays in handling customer response. In one extreme instance, a successful campaign resulted in internal complaints about the work involved in answering enquiries!

While you may not be *directly* involved with efficient follow-through, this does not absolve you of responsibility: internal marketing should ensure that all concerned are fully briefed in advance, ready to take whatever action is necessary (handling telephone enquiries, despatching literature, or following up sales leads) thus avoiding wasted effort. Incredible though it seems, one recent survey (across a wide range of product and service areas) revealed that, on average, some 90 per cent of enquiries were never followed up.

Apart from being sound practice, tactful reminders are also prudent self-defence – if sales targets are not achieved, it is always tempting for colleagues to blame poor advertising!

Workload problems can if necessary be contracted out to specialist organizations. For example, some external services not only handle telephone enquiries but also store and despatch literature on your behalf. Alternatively, subject to agreement with postal authorities, you can cite your head office or some other prestigious address in your advertisements, but have letters redirected to a different office, or perhaps a 'fulfilment house' (which stocks and posts your material for you). This can encourage response and the same time reduce administrative costs, by eliminating internal re-routing of enquiries. It also saves valuable time, thus reducing delays in responding to requests.

A note of caution is called for, however – are such costs to be charged against the advertising budget?

Your next step

With the campaign now running, the next task is to evaluate its results, to see what lessons can be learned for the future.

PART 11: Evaluation of results

The result proves the wisdom of the act.

Ovid, *Heroides,* Epis. ii, 1.65

Evaluation of results implies you have records to evaluate! Much valuable information is alas thrown into the wastepaper basket for lack of staff to both record and evaluate – yet the improvement which could be achieved would more than pay the labour costs involved, and even make a major contribution to profit!

The final planning stage of evaluating results is discussed in the next chapter.

36 Evaluating results

They know enough who know how to learn.

Henry Brooks Adams

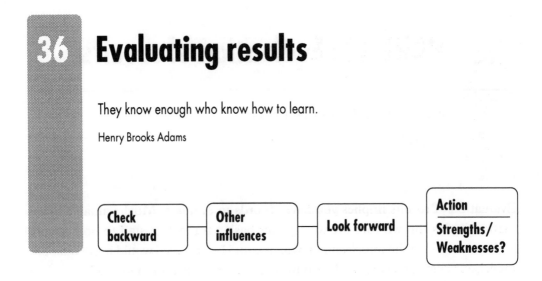

Check backward — Other influences — Look forward — Action / Strengths/Weaknesses?

Evaluating results should be approached from the four standpoints listed.

Check backward

Firstly, did all your insertions appear as scheduled, with the correct advertisements in the positions booked on the due dates? Where no special positions were specified, were your advertisements well placed, or did they compare unfavourably with competitors? Was adjacent editorial helpful or harmful? How good was printing quality, and were illustrations reproduced with true colour values?

There may be few occasions in the year when you need to take up matters with media owners, but mistakes do occur from time to time. You must therefore check voucher copies carefully and make similar checks with other media.

Other influences

You must keep careful records of happenings which, if not allowed for, would give an incorrect picture of campaign effectiveness. These should be noted under two inter-related headings:

1. Favourable or unfavourable?
Circumstances such as heatwaves will increase sales of ice cream and cold drinks, as examples. By all means bask in reflected glory as well as sunshine, but you should also record events (such as transport strikes) which adversely affect sales. Without such a record, you could perhaps find yourself unfairly blamed at some future post-mortem on disappointing sales.

2. One-off or repeat?

The two happenings just cited, if not one-off, are certainly not predictable. Other events occur regularly (perhaps on an annual basis) and, by building these into the planning process, your records ensure you gain maximum benefit in future – or perhaps take avoiding action.

Look forward

It is relevant in this context to mention the DAGMAR concept, derived from a book by Russell Colley entitled *Defining Advertising Goals for Measured Advertising Results.*

Before looking forward you should therefore (as with Campaign Approval) remind yourself of the answer to a fundamental question: 'What is your specific advertising strategy?' Was this new users, existing users, brand-switch or some other specific objective? With your goal established, you can now review various ways to evaluate advertising's contribution to achieving this objective.

1. *Ex-factory sales* With a launch campaign, wide distribution is a necessity since, if the product is not available for purchase, your efforts will be wasted. Direct mail and trade press advertising often supplement sales staff efforts, and ex-factory sales can indicate the results of this support campaign.
2. *Retail audits* Ex-factory sales indicate 'selling in' – but what if this is not followed by 'selling out', your product simply sitting on retailers' shelves? For this reason, many advertisers subscribe to retail audits of which a wide variety is available, specializing in particular product areas. In essence the operation is simple: to opening stock add deliveries during the month, take away stocks remaining at the end, and you know that month's sales. This oversimplifies, since a good audit gives much more information, including how many units are on display and where within the outlet. Also important is similar information about competitors. A good retail audit will also reveal the most popular shopping days for particular products, and even the most popular time of day. This information can directly influence media scheduling.
3. *Consumer panels* Retail audits tell if sales have risen (or fallen) but not how any increase was achieved. Was this through new users, existing users or brand-switch – vital information, depending on your objective. Many advertisers therefore subscribe to consumer panels (of which there is again a wide variety available, specializing in various product areas) which make this information available. Some panels go even further, 'fusing' with media research data to identify, for example, the television programmes watched by those who actually buy your products.

4. *Consumer surveys* Other research organizations will post-test your campaign, measuring *reading and noting* (numbers of people claiming to have seen your advertisements). Others check *impact* or recall (the degree to which your campaign actually *communicated*). You should examine incorrect recall statistics just as much as correct ones, to check brand ignorance, brand confusion and recall not proven. Also, beware of 'spurious' awareness – non-existent products have sometimes achieved high recall scores! Also, check attitudes (favourable or unfavourable) and opinions (belief versus disbelief). High recall could correlate with unfavourable image or unbelievable claims – or even both! Some research goes further, through to brand image evaluation.

5. *Direct response* Some fortunate advertisers are able to relate advertising directly to its results. As examples, many retailers, advertisers selling direct and those whose campaigns solicit coupon or telephone response. Direct response can also arise through media owners' reply services. Direct response campaigns can 'key' each insertion so that respondents indicate in which publication and on what date they saw your advertisement. Analysis of results can evaluate an important range of variables, including:

- Product offer.
- Media used.
- Area coverage.
- Type of response.
- Cost per reply.
- Conversion rate to sales.
- Purchase values.
- Advertisement unit: size – position – colour.
- Frequency.
- Timing.
- Different messages.
- Alternative expressions of same message .
- Creative life – change needed?
- Response incentives – alternative offers?
- Reply devices – coupon variations? – telephone variations?
- And, of course, combinations thereof.

Those mounting direct response campaigns are indeed in an enviable position.

Action

Whichever approach is adopted the purpose of evaluation is action, which can follow two routes:

1. *Strengths*
Evaluation of results can lead to targeting a group not covered by your original market definition but which, by responding, proved its interest. Results evaluation thus leads to changes in marketing policy rather than advertising. Alternatively, the target groups may remain unchanged, but evaluation of results improves campaign productivity by getting better results for the same money.

2. *Weaknesses*
The counterpart of 'better results for the same money' is 'same results for less money'. Elimination of weaknesses means you can use the money saved to buy what you could not afford before – and always remember that no budget is ever sufficient!

Advertisements which do not bring results are not *always* a waste of money. Depending on your viewpoint, they can also be an investment. The investment comes from finding out – the hard way – that they did not work, thus preventing further waste in future.

Closing the loop

Schedule improvement is as important as the original plan, and monitoring performance on an on-going basis as important as post-campaign assessment. This chapter completes the circular process since what you learn from evaluation of results provides the basis for future planning

Your next step

Return to Chapter 6 ('Previous activity') or perhaps Chapter 34 ('Implementing proposals') – you now have new information on which to base future messages and media.

If using external services as discussed in Appendix A, this feedback plays an equally vital role.

Either way, you should also turn to Appendix D, which comprises a blank proforma *Personal Work Sheet*, for use when planning future advertising.

En route you can consult, if appropriate:

Appendix B : Business-to-business campaigns

Appendix C: Advertising and database marketing

Appendix A: In-house or external services?

Get a reputation for paying invoices promptly. It's amazing how the most skilled creatives tend to gravitate to your office.

Daniel L. Yadin, *Creating Effective Marketing Communications*

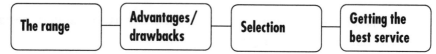

Whether undertaken in-house or through external services, the component tasks of planning successful advertising remain the same. This Appendix discusses the advantages and drawbacks of using external services, their selection, and using them to best advantage.

The range of specialist services

There is a wide variety of services available. Heading the list is the full-service advertising agency which provides – as its name implies – a full advertising service in partnership with its clients: research to assist in situation analysis, agreement on objectives, preparation of message and media proposals, and implementation. Some agencies diversify their departments beyond these essential functions, whilst others concentrate their abilities, specializing in technical or business-to-business accounts, recruitment advertising, or other areas.

Other 'agencies' concentrate their activities in a different way. Rather than provide both messages and media, they restrict their expertise to one function only, and it is thus possible to call on specialist services for creative work alone. On the media side, there are media independents which buy media on advertisers' behalf, irrespective of whichever agency or creative consultancy provides the creative work.

While many special needs have existed for years and are covered by the services of long-established companies, the swiftly-changing world of advertising means that new needs constantly arise. More often than not, new organizations set up to cater for these new needs. This Appendix, however, concentrates on advertising agencies.

The advantages and drawbacks of agency service

There are advantages and drawbacks to both in-house and agency operations. What is not immediately apparent is that one is the counterpart of the other: the advantages of agency service are the drawbacks of undertaking the work yourself. Conversely, the advantages of in-house operations are the drawbacks of external service.

Advantages
Not necessarily in order of importance, these include:

1. *An expert team* Agencies provide a team of experts, including specialists in the many different advertising tasks.
2. *The work-load problem* Clients could recruit staff direct, but what if there is insufficient work to keep a specialist fully occupied? The agency, by spreading work across a number of clients according to their needs, can afford to employ full-time specialists.

   Any advertiser who tries to overcome the work-load problem by use of free-lances has the multiple tasks of locating, evaluating, selecting, engaging, briefing and then co-ordinating independent specialists. The agency, on the other hand, has the experts readily available and already working as a team.
3. *A detached viewpoint* A third advantage is the agency's fresh approach, since staff are detached from the client's day-to-day operations. Internal staff often become so involved in detail that they fail to identify underlying problems.
4. *Other experience* Agency staff handle a number of clients, and experience gained in solving one problem is frequently applicable to others. Each client thus benefits from the agency's experience in other fields.
5. *Buying power* The agency's total expenditure necessarily exceeds that of any one client. When buying on its clients' behalf, it can thus bring financial leverage to bear on suppliers of whatever their clients need. This 'buying muscle', coupled with expert knowledge of which suppliers to approach, can result in considerable savings.
6. *Reduced costs* This particular advantage does not necessarily apply on world-wide basis but, within the UK and numerous other countries, a further advantage arises from the commission received from media owners (ranging from 10 to 15 per cent) which helps reduce the cost of agency service.

   When commission received provides sufficient profit (after covering operating costs) the agency may work on commission alone, and the advertiser reaps the benefit of agency service without charge. On the other hand, if the agency finds its expenses in handling the client's advertising exceed the commission income (or leave an insufficient margin of profit) it charges a service fee to obtain the necessary additional income. Even when the advertiser pays a service fee, however, this is often less expensive than taking experts onto his own staff. Conversely, should the client consider that commission gives the agency more than sufficient profit, he may – when negotiating arrangements – call for the commission level to be reduced. The possibility of payment on a straight fee basis is discussed below.

7. *Other savings* Other aspects of agency service can also result in welcome savings in time, effort and money. Any company mounting its campaign direct is necessarily involved in extensive clerical and administrative chores, and in paying innumerable individual invoices. Using an agency makes the client's life operationally easier, and comprehensive accounts can be settled with a single payment.

8. *Flexibility* Should an advertiser take on staff in expectation of additional work, there may be redundancy costs if the anticipated work does not materialize. Using an agency means that they, rather than the client, have the work load problem. Much the same applies to quality of work: it is relatively easier to change agencies than the staff of a department, should the advertising not match up to the standard required.

The drawbacks

For advantages there are necessarily drawbacks, although these are in most cases outweighed by the benefits. Again not necessarily in order of importance, these include:

1. *Divided attention* As agency staff work for several clients at the same time, they cannot devote full attention to all of them simultaneously. If one client faces an urgent problem, other pressure may prevent agency staff from dealing with it, whereas a manufacturer with in-house facilities knows his problems receive undivided attention all the time.

2. *The time lag* External service is often slower than direct working, and an organization subject to unexpected market changes might find it more expedient to do the job in-house. If the content, timing and destination of advertising messages are all under constant review, this could well apply.

3. *Cost* A possible drawback may arise from the relationship between commission received, service fee charged, and the work involved. Much depends on the type of advertising, for where media rates are low (as with many business publications) the agency receives little income from commission. It takes as

much effort to prepare an advertisement for a technical journal as for a national newspaper, but the former task brings less revenue, simply because the agency receives commission on a smaller sum. The commission on some types of advertising may be so small, and the service fee so high, that it becomes uneconomic to employ an agency.

4. *Built-in inertia* Income versus workload problems may extend further, since the agency receives roughly the same commission on a given sum, whether spent on a limited number of large advertisements in a few media or numerous small insertions in an extended range, but its operating costs vary considerably.

   The same argument applies to changes in message content. The agency incurs lower costs by preparing one advertisement and letting it run for a year than if it prepares a series, or changes the message each month. The commission income remains the same, yet monthly copy changes mean 12 times as much work, with consequent higher staff costs and lower profits.

   The commission system thus presents a built-in temptation for agencies to achieve maximum income for minimum effort.

   Agencies rightly need to make a profit, and charging a higher service fee could recoup the additional costs involved. The higher the service fee, however, the more attractive it is for clients to run in-house departments, or transfer to a rival agency charging a lower fee.

Agency directors are well aware of these drawbacks, and take positive action to overcome them. Equally, responsibility rests also with clients: possible drawbacks should be ironed out at selection stage, and client-agency relationships be compatible. The answer, of course, is for agencies to charge a just fee, arrived at by negotiation with clients. As already mentioned, the possibility of payment on a straight fee basis is discussed below.

Selecting external services

There are a number of important considerations to bear in mind when selecting external services. Not necessarily in strict order of importance, these include:

1. *Services provided* This is largely a cross-checking procedure – what services are needed, and which does the agency provide? There should be a close match because, if the agency lacks any necessary service, the problem then arises of locating, evaluating, selecting, engaging, briefing and then co-ordinating independent freelance workers.

2. *Quality of work* The standard of services provided is as important as the range. Quality evaluation is a skilled task, to which Chapter 33 ('The correct criteria') was devoted.

3. *Quality of staff* Quality of work depends on quality of staff, and it is advisable to consider staffing *in depth*. The client may meet top management from time to time, but who will actually handle the account, and how can the client ensure his affairs are not delegated to the most junior junior?

4. *Relevant experience* A major advantage of external service lies in experience in other fields. When selecting an agency, do staff have relevant experience from which the client can benefit?

5. *Accounts handled* Experience in other fields arises through the agency's accounts as much as staff. Client lists should be reviewed under three headings:

   a) *Relevant* – the agency may handle accounts which, although not competitive, give invaluable knowledge of the target market, and practical working experience of media which reach them.

   b) *Competitive* – this is controversial, as some advertisers rule out employing any agency handling a competing account. Others look at the agency's operating structure, since it may function on a Group system whereby it divides into autonomous self-contained service units, as discussed below.

   c) *Other* – many client lists, in the broadest sense, make impressive reading, comprising leading companies which demand (and presumably receive) a high standard of service.

6. *Organizational structure* Some agencies are organized on a 'pyramid' system, whereby contact executives are responsible for clients (rather than staff members) and the agency's specialists all work on several accounts, each of which may be supervised by a different client service director.

   Other agencies operate on a Group system, dividing into two or more units, each amounting to a self-contained service operation. The system has various advantages: it permits the handling of competing clients, each account group becomes a profit centre, it encourages a competitive spirit, and staff can be switched between groups from time to time to bring fresh input whilst still maintaining continuity

7. *Size of agency and importance of client's account* These two criteria should be reviewed together, and either of two extremes avoided. If an account is too small by the agency's standards then, when different clients compete for attention, big spenders may receive priority. Equally, it is best to avoid being too big, since one advantage of external service is a detached viewpoint, which sometimes necessitates drawing attention to unwelcome home truths. If a client

accounts for too high a proportion of total billing, this may inhibit plain speaking for fear of upsetting the client and thereby losing the business.

8. *Operating arrangements* Practical arrangements for handling the client's business are important, as the frequency, duration and location of meetings directly affect operating costs. And which agency staff will work on the account? Furthermore, is it agency practice to issue contact reports after each meeting, summarizing the decisions taken, allocating responsibilities and specifying dates? Open discussion well in advance about working arrangements saves time-wasting arguments later.

9. *Cost* This must of course be considered in light of the amount of work together with its quality but, whatever the commission and/or service fee arrangements, it is essential there is a clear understanding between both parties as to precisely what is (and what is not) covered by the agency's remuneration.

   A further possibility is payment on a straight fee basis. There are three main types of fee arrangements:

   a) *Hourly rates* where the time spent by agency staff is charged to the client at varying rates. Overall control ensures that the charge to client does not exceed an agreed amount.

   b) *Retainer fee* where the client pays a standard monthly fee, irrespective of the time spent. More work is done in some months and less in others, but a satisfactory balance achieved over the year. The agency benefits from a consistent cash flow, and clients must of course ensure they get value for money.

   c) *Payment by results* An agreed minimum fee is paid to cover operating expenses, and agency profit depends on reaching agreed targets. The problem with such arrangements lies in assessing the agency contribution.

10. *Terms of contract* As legalities are important, the best advice is to read and agree the small print. Who owns the copyright of advertisements? How frequently will accounts be presented, and with what conditions of payment? Is advance payment required to cover operating costs? What costs are indeed covered – see point 9. Many arguments can be avoided by a clear understanding of such matters. Finally, should working relationships prove unsatisfactory, what notice must either party give to terminate the contract?

11. *Informed opinions* Informal contact with those having practical experience of the agency's service (this could include other clients, media representatives, printers or other suppliers) can yield useful information. But do remember the old adage – *No client is ever satisfied!* If all report adversely, however, then dissatisfaction may be far deeper than with the minor snags which necessarily crop up in all working relationships.

12. *Professional membership* Whilst there is nothing to prevent someone with no real knowledge proclaiming himself an 'advertising agent', it is very different to claim membership of relevant professional organizations, which lay down stringent standards before accepting firms into membership.

Most will also assist intending clients select an advertising agency by suggesting a shortlist of suitable members. From that point on, responsibility necessarily rests with the client: it is essential to meet agency staff, ensure both parties to the contract are compatible, and agree how best to work in partnership.

Getting the best service

A. How not to do it . . .

The preamble to Part 6 outlined some classic errors:

1. *Meaningless non-instructions* – requesting eye-catching, attractive, arresting and memorable campaigns.
2. *Pre-empting the solution* – by specifying in advance what you expect.

When the agency presents its proposals, further mistakes to avoid are:

3. *Rejecting the pre-judged unexpected* – 'That's not what I expected: I thought I would see Message A delivered through Media B.' Which is simply the second error recycled!
4. *Approval 'on the nod'* Agency proposals represent many hours of concentrated work but, if accepted without question, staff may well ask themselves 'Why bother?' As all people are advertising 'experts', creative proposals are invariably discussed (even if by incorrect criteria!), so this comment applies particularly to media proposals. Scheduling involved calculating innumerable alternatives, and then evaluating them to select the best, so why no questions?

   Remember that agency staff have many demands on their time and, should you be considered 'a soft touch', your account may not receive as much attention in the future.
5. *Being awkward* Innumerable niggling arguments about minor points of detail are not conducive to an atmosphere in which the agency can give of its best. Invoices should of course be checked and, if necessary, queried – but not at a meeting called expressly to present new message and media proposals!

B. How best to . . .

The best route to getting the best service is:

1. *Procedural agreement* Thoroughly discuss detailed working arrangements in advance, to ensure smooth operations and minimize subsequent time-wasting.
2. *Give a good briefing* Although there are as many methods as there are people, most agree that a good brief comprises:
   a) Situation analysis
   b) Objective
   c) Budget.
   The preamble to Part 6 stated clearly 'First define the problem – then turn to the next planning stage: preparation of proposals to achieve the defined objective, within the constraints of the budget.' Give the agency the problem – not the solution.
3. *Give sufficient time* Don't expect the agency's best work tomorrow!
4. *Come to the presentation with an open mind.* The need for such an approach is now, hopefully, self-evident. Be prepared for the unexpected!
5. *Ask searching questions* Rather than accepting proposals 'on the nod' or spending so much time on minor queries that you fail to focus on media and messages, ask searching questions which keep agency staff on their toes – most people respond to a *positive* challenge!
6. *Reach swift decisions* While it is important to scrutinize proposals meticulously, it is equally important to do so swiftly. Early approval gives more time for execution, thus preventing the costly mistakes which so often occur with rush jobs. Delay can also result in missed deadlines – what a waste of money if you have no advertisements to appear in the spaces for which you are legally liable to pay! Swift approval can also lead to cost savings: undue delay may mean you find all the best positions already booked, and have to bid at a high rate for the few remaining spaces!
7. *Give feedback* It is equally important to let agency staff know the results of their efforts. Many complain of initial feedback from clients about campaigns mounted on their behalf. Without such information, how can the agency improve future advertising effectiveness?

In short, help the agency give of its best by working in partnership.

Agencies too have their own approaches to achieving the best working relationships. One leading agency, for example, adopts what amounts to a four-stage process:

1. *At situation analysis stage:* We think we understand your problem – do you think we understand it? If not, let's ensure we do.
2. *At objective stage:* Are we agreed on your specific objective, which is . . . Sign here!
3. *At strategy stage:* Before we devote our time (and your money!) to preparing proposals, do we agree that the single-minded proposition which will achieve your objective is . . . Sign here!

Only after these three stages are agreed does attention turn to detailed creative proposals, and media schedules to deliver them.

4. *Tactics*   When message and media proposals are presented, this is done in context of objective and strategy. Attention thus focuses on:
   a) Has the single-minded proposition been made to come alive in a compelling way?
   b) Will it be delivered by the best possible media schedule?.

Another leading agency adopts a POMMMM model, focusing on Product, Objectives, Market, Media, Message, Measurement. Although not included in the acronym, this agency's model also includes a fifth M – Money!

A final salutary quotation (from my earlier books) is:

> If you tell your agency that the brief is 'the same as last year' then you should either resign or fire the agency, since 'no change' means that all the time, effort and money spent on advertising has apparently had no effect whatsoever!

Appendix B:
Business-to-business campaigns

This book is about the organization man . . . I can think of no other way to describe the people I am talking about. They are not the workers, nor are they the white-collar people in the usual, clerk sense of the word. These people only work for the organization. The ones I am talking about belong to it as well.

William H. Whyte, *The Organization Man*

The four p's — People — Purchasing patterns

Business-to-business marketing was, until recently, known as industrial marketing but the term 'industrial' is too restrictive. Business-to-business is more accurate, and covers both products and services, marketed to a range of organizations far wider then manufacturing industry. Within this Appendix, however, the term 'industrial' may be used interchangeably with 'business-to-business' or the shorter 'business' marketing, for simplicity.

Conventional marketing concentrates on the traditional four p's of *product, price, place* and *promotion*. More sophisticated analysis suggests that business marketing demands two new p's:

* People.
* Purchasing patterns.

The four p's

Even these differ for business-to-business marketing.

* *Product* – whilst there are services as such, many industrial products are product *and* service – so complex they can not be purchased without expert advice. Furthermore, many are in what economists describe as 'derived demand' – they are components, demand for which derives from demand for the main product into which they are incorporated.

- *Price* – rather than a fixed price which can be cited in advertisements, business-to-business operations may necessitate submission of quotations, negotiations about finance, and even leasing or contract hire.
- *Place* – most business products are sold direct or through appointed agents or distributors, in contrast with the indirect selling of consumer products through wholesalers and retailers.
- *Promotion* – budgets are usually smaller and campaigns feature rational rather than emotional messages, which appear in different (and lower cost) media.

People

This first new 'p' acknowledges that business marketing is not solely concerned with manipulating the traditional four p's, but more with developing a critical network of person-to-person relationships. Furthermore, these are long-term interactive relationships – contrast this with relatively straightforward repeat purchases of consumer merchandise.

A. External people
Target market executives merit analysis from various standpoints:

1. *Target people* Chapter 4 established that business markets are defined by occupation and industry rather than conventional demographics. The point made here is that the way these executives operate within their firms has direct implications for advertising messages and media.
2. *Purchasing people* Rather than individual purchases, business-to-business marketing involves committee decisions taken by the decision-making units discussed below.
3. *Partnership people* Many industrial products are produced and used in an inter-active relationship between user and supplier. The potential purchaser's ability to brief you on technical requirements is as important as your ability to design and manufacture the product.
4. *Multi-structure people* The organization to which you hope to sell may function in separate operating divisions. Sometimes these are autonomous and amount to different target markets, each calling for individual campaigns. Some large organizations, on the other hand, divide internally into individual profit centres. Should you target these operational units or some central service division? If the latter, what are their respective terms of reference?
5. *Cross-company people* Many top businessmen hold non-executive directorships in different companies. Their opinion of your efficiency in servicing one

organization can directly influence the likelihood of your getting a contract from another.

6. *Ex-market people* For some industrial purchases, the real decision is not what to buy nor which supplier to buy from, but whether the project is to proceed. This in turn may be determined by government views about the project's effects on the economy. Until the decision to proceed is taken, the would-be purchasing organization has no authority to buy, and there is little hope of an order.

B. Internal people

In-company staff demand equally careful analysis, since they comprise a very expensive resource and, in many respects, *are* the company.

1. *Service people* This simply recognizes a point already established: an organization may provide a product *and*/or service, the latter having major implications.
2. *Two-businesses people* To operate successfully, your staff must be experts in customers' businesses as well as their own. Unless they fully understand customers' problems, and can communicate with them in their own language, there is little prospect of an order.
3. *In-depth people* In business marketing there are multi-facet sellers just as much as buyers. Sales is just one of many departments of your organization from which various employees may be in contact with their counterparts in different sections of the buying organization.
4. *Multi-structure people* In the same way that purchasers break their activities into separate profit-centre operations, so do suppliers. All too often, however, this leads to fragmented effort. At worst, conflicting activities are counter-productive, undermining each other's effectiveness. Alternatively, the various campaigns are merely self-contained and lack a synergistic approach whereby careful co-ordination increases their individual effectiveness and thus that of the overall campaign.
5. *Partnership people* Just as your product is produced in an interactive relationship with customers, there are equally important relationships with your suppliers or sub-contractors. Their ability to supply depends on your participative approach.
6. *Production people* In extreme cases, where management is 'production-oriented', the marketing problem is an internal one, convincing the Board that advertising is a vital activity, calling for expenditure of time and effort as well as money. Hopefully, such cases will be few!

Even when management is more enlighted, there is still need for 'internal marketing'. At simplest level, this involves keeping representatives informed about promotional activity, which they can use as an effective sales tool when making client contact.

Frequently, however, internal marketing is far more complex – particularly when there are multiple contacts between numerous in-house individuals and their counterparts within customers' firms. Where your own organization operates in autonomous divisions, there is even greater need for internal marketing on 'Project management' lines, to ensure each division is aware of the activities of the others, and their joint efforts co-ordinated to maximum effect.

C. Permanent people
These contacts between and within internal and external people are continuing relationships. Once a purchaser has established a relationship with a supplier, the purchased products are expected to contribute dependably to the purchaser's performance over long periods of time. There is therefore need for two distinct but inter-related and continuous campaigns – one aimed at target markets, and another at your own staff.

Purchasing patterns

To facilitate advertising analysis, construct 'Buy-grids' which must reflect five important aspects of buyer behaviour, if you are to advertise successfully. These are Buy-types, Buy-classes, Buy-roles, Buy-motives, and Buy-stages.

Before addressing this new material, however, remind yourself of earlier discussion of Purchasing Profiles and Buy-scales on page 52 – most business purchases involve rational, pre-planned, high involvement consultative decisions. Whether they are regular, frequent or brand loyal depends on circumstances.

Innovation/Diffusion, discussed earlier on page 53, also has important implications for business products. When launching new techological developments, innovators are not only important in their own right but serve as multipliers in spreading the word to others.

1. Buy-types
Most industrial purchases can be categorized under one of three headings:

a) *The industrial market:* organizations which acquire goods or services for the production of other goods and services.
b) *The reseller market:* organizations which acquire goods to sell or hire to others at a profit.

c) *The public service market:* government units, national or local, which purchase or hire goods or services to perform their due function.

The three market types (and sub-sections thereof) have very different buying motives, calling for different messages as well as different media to deliver them. Within each buy-type, any organization might proceed to one of three buy-classes.

2. Buy-classes
Most industrial purchases can again be categorized under three headings:

a) *Straight rebuy* – whereby re-ordering occurs with no change in specification, perhaps with 'automatic re-order' stock control systems. Providing product performance remains satisfactory, it is very difficult for a rival supplier to disrupt the sequence. Advertising can play a significant role in maintaining source loyalty for the current supplier, whereas competitors' advertising could give compelling reasons for switching supply sources.

b) *Modified rebuy* – when there is a change in purchase criteria. The buyer's needs may have altered, or perhaps revised supplier specifications led to re-examination. Advertising can deliver vital new information about changes in price or product performance, leading to the decision to re-examine.

c) *New purchase* – where firms consider products or services not previously purchased. Advertising may play different roles here – one is to channel a prospect's need into an enquiry and then into an order. Alternatively the task might be educational, awakening an unrecognized need. Advertising's dual function then is to stimulate latent demand *and* channel it towards your company – you will not win medals for increasing competitors' sales!

Whatever the buy-class, a number of different individuals will be involved in the purchasing decision.

3. Buy-roles
Most industrial purchases are made by teams (formal or informal) and it is important to identify members of the 'DMU' or decision-making unit. Various roles have been suggested, including:

a) *Initiators* – those who perceive (or can be made to recognize) their need for a product or service.

b) *Users* – those who will actually use the product or service, and may play an important part in defining purchase specifications.

c) *Influencers* – those who influence decisions, either directly or indirectly.

d) *Buyers* – those with formal authority for negotiating and placing orders. They may also advise on specifications, and perhaps select suppliers. In many organizations, purchasing is recognized as a professional function.

e) *Deciders* – those with formal or informal power to select the final supplier. For relatively minor purchases, buyers may also be deciders, but crucial decisions are usually taken at Board level.

f) *Specifiers* – those identifying a need, and specifying the type of product to satisfy that need. Specifiers include technical specialists who specify components in general terms without naming a particular brand or supplier. The latter task is often left to buyers.

g) *Gate-keepers* – individuals who control the flow of information to DMU members, and may block message delivery.

This complex situation is made even more difficult by the fact that the executives occupying each role in a given organization are likely to change from one purchasing decision to the next.

Different members of the DMU may have different motives as well as different roles.

4. *Buy-motives*

There are two questions to ask, already discussed in Chapter 17:

a) *What are your target market buying?* This is not necessarily what you think you are selling!

b) *What is their buying perspective?* By what criteria do they choose between one supplier and another?

As with consumer advertising, these questions have clear implications for message content. Whatever the motives, purchasers may be at different stages of the buying process.

5. *Buy-stages*

It is important to establish the potential customer's position on the 'purchasing scale', since industrial purchases pass through several stages including:

a) *Problem recognition* – identification, anticipation or recognition of need, and general need description.

b) *Product specification* – establishing the precise characteristics of the items needed.

c) *Supplier search* – locating potential suitable suppliers.

d) *Proposal solicitation* – contact with candidate suppliers, to request proposals.

e) *Supplier selection* – evaluation of alternative offers.

f) *Decide/buy* – make final choice and agree order routine.

g) *Use* – install and operate.

h) *Post-purchase review* – and evaluation.

Clearly you must decide at which stage (or stages) advertising should contribute. Is its role awakening a prospect organization to a need of which it is unaware? Alternatively, if already at the 'supplier search' stage, the advertising task is to ensure inclusion on the short list. Or is this a case where the ATR (Awareness, Trial and Reinforcement) model applies?

Notes:

1. These grids are not intended as a formal analysis procedure, but only as trigger concepts to stimulate your planning process.

2. The buy-groupings are not exclusive, but may overlap.

3. Like any checklist, this approach is an aid to thought: not a substitute for it!

The time-lag

Because of the technical complexities involved, business buying decisions require more information, and often involve more uncertainty about product performance, necessitating longer evaluation periods. This often means significant time-lags between the application of advertising effort and obtaining a buying response.

Promotional planning

Analysis of these inter-related buy-aspects is made more complex by the fact that each individual buying organization is likely to differ significantly from every other. Accordingly, advertising planning might necessitate viewing each existing or potential purchaser as a separate target market. Hence the importance of the database approach, discussed in Appendix C. Few (if any) consumer goods companies must be so concerned about tailoring strategies to each individual customer.

A final note

Although advertising to business markets may be difficult, it is often easier to evaluate results. Suppliers are in contact with existing and potential customers, either direct or through distributors or agents, and have more feedback about their efforts. Business marketers who complain how difficult it is to mount campaigns should spare a thought for consumer colleagues with no direct customer contact: they sell to wholesalers or retailers who then resell to ultimate purchasers. To find out who these ultimate purchasers are, or how effective their advertising has been, they must undertake massive market research – in some cases the research expenditure involved often exceeds many business advertising budgets. Consumer companies are often envious of business firms' direct customer feedback.

Feedback and tailoring strategy to each individual customer are both discussed in Appendix C, which examines advertising and database marketing.

Appendix C: Advertising and database marketing

People have one thing in common: they are all different.

Robert Zend

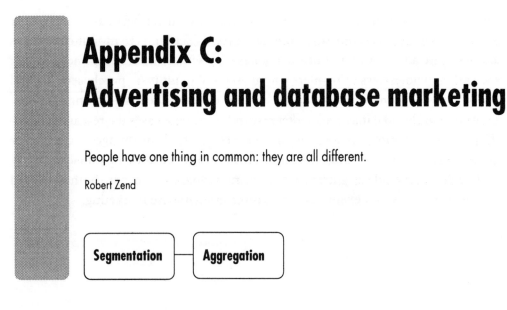

Segmentation — **Aggregation**

Conventional advertising achieves segmentation by 'desegregating' large markets into smaller groups, whereas database marketing segments the opposite way – by aggregating individual customer records.

The new concept is rooted in the old philosophy of getting closer to your market. Identify your customers, understand and meet their needs, and treat them well, and in turn you will do well even in a highly competitive environment – and database marketing is simply a sophisticated means of meeting this objective. Its principles apply particularly to direct mail advertising, since new technology now permits personalized individual messages tailored to database information. The principles are nevertheless equally applicable to other aspects of marketing, with results fed into the same database.

Database marketing can take potential new customers up a five-rung 'Ladder of Loyalty', leading them through different market stages:

1. *Suspects* – potential customers who have not yet indicated interest in your product or service, but merit a 'cold' campaign.
2. *Prospects* – those who have indicated interest, but not yet purchased.
3. *Customers* – those who have purchased.
4. *Loyal customers* – those who buy regularly.
5. *Advocates* – those beyond passive brand loyalty, who actively recommend you to others.

The final planning stage, evaluation of results, applies particularly to database marketing. Advertising can result in off-the-page sales (or enquiries that serve as sales leads) which in turn permit retrieval systems far more sophisticated than simply recording cash sales or enquiries, and enquiries converted into orders. The database should not only specify goods sold but also analyse purchases in R, F and V (Recency, Frequency and Value) terms, as well as by conventional data such as occupation and industry or age, sex, socio-economic group, and geodemographic classification, and location. These details, fed back into the database, then serve as an integrated information system.

Database marketing is not just a means of communication, but rather a new way of defining supplier/customer/advertising relationships. It is also a new way of doing business that provides management information: database marketing could replace conventional market research through advertising campaigns (perhaps planned on the shotgun principle) which seek and measure customer response. By mapping trends, database marketing helps ensure opportunities are swiftly identified, and speeds up the process of neutralizing threats. The system can also provide management ratios such as advertising expenditure to enquiries, enquiries converted into sales, and average order value. It can further help evaluate both media and messages.

The database approach thus serves as a functional basis for management and marketing planning, sales-force control and telemarketing, just as much as for advertising, created media, direct mail, public relations and other promotional activities. It can also help co-ordinate these separate activities so that all interlock to maximum effect.

Appendix D: A personal work sheet

SUCCESSFUL ADVERTISING:

As an aid to thought (and not a substitute for it!) photocopy and complete this proforma, before starting any new advertising assignment.

Product/service

Key characteristics – physical and emotional _____

What does it actually do? – single or multi-use?_____

Individualized or family branding? _____

Competitive analysis – how different? _____

Market segments

Demographics? (= media) _____

Psychographics (= message)_____

Non vs light vs medium vs heavy users? _____

Decision process?_____

Pareto 80/20 vs shotgun? _____

Specific objective

New vs existing vs brand-switch or ? _____

Constraints

Internal – if any _____

External?_____

Budget

Amount_____

Period _____

Coverage _____

Method _____

Contingency reserve _____

Campaign requirement

Single advertisement _____

– or series _____

KEY ALTERNATIVE APPROACHES

There is no point in polishing the incorrect message.
Insist on your right to be read.
Double-check follow-through arrangements.
Define the criteria by which you will know if your campaign has succeeded.

Message

Now turn your campaign objective into a *communication* objective – what must you say to e.g. persuade people to switch brands?

Creative intention

– Your campaign will achieve its objective if your target market thinks/feels/believes

WHAT?_____

Single-minded proposition?

– benefit/brand image/key attribute/promise or U S P?_____

What are people buying?_____

– vs what you are selling _____

Buyer's perspective?_____

– why from you vs competition?_____

Substantiation?_____

Desired response? _____

Made to come alive? How?_____

Logical layout? _____

Effective typography? _____

Media

Candidate media? _____

Case-rate spending – reflect or reject?_____

Basic variables priority? – unit, duration, frequency, media list_____

Other variables?

– multiple-size campaign_____

– drip vs burst_____

Cumulative coverage _____

Frequency distribution? _____

Overall planning

Flexible execution/evaluation? _____

This campaign's relationship to others? _____

Corporate communications _____

– synergism & cross-references across all marketing communications

Index